DATE DUE

Understanding World History

The Decade of the 2000s

David Robson

Bruno Leone
Series Consultant

ReferencePoint Press®

San Diego, CA

© 2012 ReferencePoint Press, Inc.
Printed in the United States

For more information, contact:
ReferencePoint Press, Inc.
PO Box 27779
San Diego, CA 92198
www.ReferencePointPress.com

LIBRARY OF CONGRESS CATALOGING-IN-PUBLICATION DATA

Robson, David, 1966–
  The decade of the 2000s / by David Robson.
    p. cm. — (Understanding world history series)
  Includes bibliographical references and index.
  ISBN-13: 978-1-60152-187-3 (hardback)
  ISBN-10: 1-60152-187-1 (hardback)
  1. History, Modern—21st century—Juvenile literature. 2. Civilization, Modern—21st century—Juvenile literature. I. Title.
  D862.R63 2012
  909.83—dc22

                                                                          2010052489

Contents

Foreword

When the Puritans first emigrated from England to America in 1630, they believed that their journey was blessed by a covenant between themselves and God. By the terms of that covenant they agreed to establish a community in the New World dedicated to what they believed was the true Christian faith. God, in turn, would reward their fidelity by making certain that they and their descendants would always experience his protection and enjoy material prosperity. Moreover, the Lord guaranteed that their land would be seen as a shining beacon—or in their words, a "city upon a hill"—which the rest of the world would view with admiration and respect. By embracing this notion that God could and would shower his favor and special blessings upon them, the Puritans were adopting the providential philosophy of history—meaning that history is the unfolding of a plan established or guided by a higher intelligence.

The concept of intercession by a divine power is only one of many explanations of the driving forces of world history. Historians and philosophers alike have subscribed to numerous other ideas. For example, the ancient Greeks and Romans argued that history is cyclical. Nations and civilizations, according to these ancients of the Western world, rise and fall in unpredictable cycles; the only certainty is that these cycles will persist throughout an endless future. The German historian Oswald Spengler (1880–1936) echoed the ancients to some degree in his controversial study *The Decline of the West.* Spengler asserted that all civilizations inevitably pass through stages comparable to the life span of a person: childhood, youth, adulthood, old age, and, eventually, death. As the title of his work implies, Western civilization is currently entering its final stage.

Joining those who see purpose and direction in history are thinkers who completely reject the idea of meaning or certainty. Rather, they reason that since there are far too many random and unseen factors at work on the earth, historians would be unwise to endorse historical predictability of any type. Warfare (both nuclear and conventional), plagues, earthquakes, tsunamis, meteor showers, and other catastrophic world-changing events have loomed large throughout history and prehistory. In his essay "A Free Man's Worship," philosopher and mathematician Bertrand Russell (1872–1970) supported this argument, which many refer to as the nihilist or chaos theory of history. According to Russell, history follows no preordained path. Rather, the earth itself and all life on earth resulted from, as Russell describes it, an "accidental collocation of atoms." Based on this premise, he pessimistically concluded that all human achievement will eventually be "buried beneath the debris of a universe in ruins."

Whether history does or does not have an underlying purpose, historians, journalists, and countless others have nonetheless left behind a record of human activity tracing back nearly 6,000 years. From the dawn of the great ancient Near Eastern civilizations of Mesopotamia and Egypt to the modern economic and military behemoths China and the United States, humanity's deeds and misdeeds have been and continue to be monitored and recorded. The distinguished British scholar Arnold Toynbee (1889–1975), in his widely acclaimed 12-volume work entitled *A Study of History*, studied 21 different civilizations that have passed through history's pages. He noted with certainty that others would follow.

In the final analysis, the academic and journalistic worlds mostly regard history as a record and explanation of past events. From a more practical perspective, history represents a sequence of building blocks—cultural, technological, military, and political—ready to be utilized and enhanced or maligned and perverted by the present. What that means is that all societies—whether advanced civilizations or preliterate tribal cultures—leave a legacy for succeeding generations to either embrace or disregard.

Recognizing the richness and fullness of history, the ReferencePoint Press Understanding World History series fosters an evaluation and interpretation of history and its influence on later generations. Each volume in the series approaches its subject chronologically and topically, with specific focus on nations, periods, or pivotal events. Primary and secondary source quotations are included, along with complete source notes and suggestions for further research.

Moreover, the series reflects the truism that the key to understanding the present frequently lies in the past. With that in mind, each series title concludes with a legacy chapter that highlights the bonds between past and present and, more important, demonstrates that world history is a continuum of peoples and ideas, sometimes hidden but there nonetheless, waiting to be discovered by those who choose to look.

Important Events of the 2000s

2002
Terrorists set off three bombs on the island of Bali in Indonesia, killing 202 people; long distance phone giant Worldcom files for bankruptcy, despite having defrauded $4 billion from its investors.

2000
The former of head of the KGB, Vladimir Putin, is elected president of Russia; terrorists attack the USS *Cole* in Yemen, killing 17 people.

2003
US armed forces invade Iraq, overthrowing dictator Saddam Hussein and unleashing chaos in that country.

2000 **2001** **2002** **2003** **2004**

2001
On September 11, nearly 3,000 people are killed when terrorists hijack four passenger airplanes and attack the World Trade Center in New York City and the Pentagon in Washington, DC; Apple introduces the iPod, transforming the music industry.

2004
A powerful earthquake in the Asian Pacific sets off a tsunami that kills hundreds of thousands of people; Gay marriage is legalized in Massachusetts.

2008

Worldwide recession begins, causing a downturn in stock markets and a collapse of the US housing market; in Mumbai, India, Islamic militants kill 164 people and wound more than 300 others; Barack Obama is elected forty-fourth president of the United States.

2005

In August, Hurricanes Katrina and Ike sweep into the Gulf Coast, submerging the city of New Orleans, killing 1,833, and leaving thousands more homeless all along the Gulf Coast; In April, Pope John Paul II dies and is succeeded by Joseph Ratzinger, who becomes Pope Benedict XVI.

2009

In June, the World Health Organization announces that the swine flu outbreak has become a pandemic; the Dow Jones industrial average closes at its lowest point in years, and investors lose billions of dollars.

2005   2006   2007   2008   2009   2010

2006

Former Iraqi president Saddam Hussein is executed by hanging; Twitter, a new electronic communication method, is introduced to the public.

2010

On January 12, a massive earthquake devastates Haiti, killing 230,000 people and leaving thousands more homeless; the *Deepwater Horizon* oil drilling platform explodes in the Gulf of Mexico, killing 11 workers and resulting in the largest oil spill in history.

2007

Former prime minister of Pakistan Benazir Bhutto is assassinated on December 27 after greeting her supporters at a rally; in June, the first iPhone goes on sale.

Introduction

The Defining Characteristics of the 2000s

The 2000s was a decade that began in fear and ended in meltdown. Dogged by terrorism, natural disasters, and economic meltdown, this 10-year period also challenged people around the world to confront extremism, climate change, and poverty in new and better ways. A *Time* magazine article published in late 2009 put it more bluntly, labeling the 2000s the "Decade from Hell." "The first 10 years of this century," writes reporter Andy Serwer, "will very likely go down as the most dispiriting and disillusioning decade Americans have lived through in the post–World War II era."[1]

In the minds of many the new millennium will be forever tied to the attacks of September 11, 2001, when Muslim extremists hijacked four airplanes, crashed them into buildings in New York and Washington, DC, and killed nearly 3,000 people. Millions watched the tragedy unfold on television, and in the coming months and years the United States went to war in Afghanistan and Iraq in response.

In other nations, political turmoil and violence had long been a fact of life. In the Middle East, the ongoing conflict between Israelis and Palestinians showed no signs of abating. Clouding any potential path to peace was the Islamic Republic of Iran, which threatened its neighbors by seeking nuclear power, perhaps even weapons. In Asia, North Korean leader Kim Jong Il already possessed nuclear warheads—as many as a dozen—and as his own country starved, he clung to power through acts

The decade of the 2000s will forever be remembered in the United States as the decade in which a terrorist attack on American soil killed thousands. Among the targets struck on September 11, 2001, was New York's World Trade Center, pictured here just moments before the twin towers collapsed.

of defiance. Meanwhile, violent conflicts in the Democratic Republic of Congo, South Ossetia in Georgia, Nigeria, Sri Lanka, Darfur, and Mexico compelled world bodies such as the United Nations (UN) and disaster relief organizations to become more vigilant in protecting human rights. Still, misunderstanding and intolerance persisted. In 2005 protests, threats, and murder followed the publication of 12 editorial cartoons in Denmark depicting the Islamic prophet Muhammad; in 2007 former Pakistani prime minister Benazir Bhutto was assassinated at a political rally when a bomb exploded near her car.

Gathering Storms

Natural disasters wreaked havoc across the globe. Parts of Indonesia, Thailand, and Sri Lanka were swept away in a massive tsunami. New Orleans, Louisiana, and parts of Mississippi were flooded in the aftermath of Hurricanes Katrina and Rita; slow government response compounded the tragedies. China and India suffered massive earthquakes that killed tens of thousands and brought down entire cities.

Economic highs and lows were also a consistent factor in the 2000s. In the United States, the median household income fell from $52,500 in 2000 to $50,303 in 2008. By 2009 the American stock market was down 26 percent from 2000. At the start of the decade, 11.3 percent of Americans lived in poverty; by 2008 that percentage had climbed to 13.2. In the East, China became an economic juggernaut, building high-rises in record time, putting millions of its poor to work, and challenging the world to match its growing financial might.

The European Union (EU), an economic and political merger of 27 nations meant to rival the power of the United States, expanded its reach. The EU's currency, the Euro, quickly became the second most traded currency after the US dollar. But, like so many nations, EU members also struggled to fight terrorism, particularly after deadly bombings in England and Spain. "This has not been a good decade for anyone overly sensitive to bad news,"[2] writes journalist Joel Achenbach.

Reasons for Hope

But all was not pain and hardship in the new millennium. Scientists made breakthroughs in discovering the mysteries of genetics, and they advocated the use of embryonic stem cells to cure diseases such as Alzheimer's. Technology, too, grew in new and exciting ways. Computers got faster and smaller; the advent of MP3 files and the iPod made music more portable; and cell phones became smart devices that provided users with access to their e-mail, the latest weather reports, or even reviews on the new Italian restaurant around the corner.

This revolution in technology also influenced the world of politics, when a senator harnessed the power of social networks such as Facebook to build a following that helped him in 2008 become the first African American president. Yet mired in social and economic crises that extended from Peru to Japan, from Russia to Ghana, people around the world could only wonder whether one nation's ability to overcome its dark racial past could influence and inspire their own struggles for peace and prosperity in the new millennium.

Chapter 1

What Events Led into the 2000s?

"What's past is prologue,"[3] says playwright William Shakespeare in his seventeenth-century drama *The Tempest*. Put another, less poetic way, what happened before will likely influence what is to come. The last decade of the twentieth century, the 1990s, set the tone and sowed the historical seeds of the new millennium. It marked the breakup of the Soviet Union, witnessed the rise of grunge music and the cloning of sheep, and included revolutions in technology and the media. Around the world, religious extremism and terrorism cast a shadow over the lives of ordinary people. And like all periods of time, the nineties ended with an excess of unfinished business for the decade yet to come.

War in the Gulf

During the previous decade—the 1980s—the United States had spent billions of dollars to support the regime of Iraqi dictator Saddam Hussein against a common enemy: Iran. By the early 1990s Hussein seemed intent on acquiring nuclear weapons and building his army into a potent fighting force, both of which made US president George H.W. Bush nervous.

The Iraqis, meanwhile, believed that their neighbor Kuwait and the United States were conspiring to drive down gas prices at the pump and destroy Iraq's economy. Hussein chose to attack Kuwait. In the summer of 1990 he ordered 30,000 of his elite Republican Guard to the border between Iraq and Kuwait; on August 2, Iraqi soldiers began shooting at Kuwaiti border guards. According to Iraq's then foreign minister Tariq

Aziz, "Iraq had no choice but to act, either to be destroyed, to be suffocated and strangled inside its territory or attack the enemy on the outside."[4] The Gulf War had begun.

Many Arab nations were surprised by Hussein's bold action and vowed to help expel Iraqi forces from Kuwait. "For us, it was shocking," said

Iraqi dictator Saddam Hussein (pictured here in 1991) ordered his forces to invade neighboring Kuwait in 1990. An international force led by the United States quickly liberated Kuwait but left the Iraqi dictator in power.

Egyptian president Hosni Mubarak. "I couldn't believe that this could happen in the Arab world."[5] The UN condemned the invasion and imposed a trade embargo on Iraq. A day later Saudi Arabia, a wealthy supplier of much of the world's oil and Kuwait's next-door neighbor, pleaded with the United States to become involved. United States forces, many already based in the Middle East, arrived in Saudi Arabia two days later. Other nations, including Great Britain, France, Egypt, Kuwait, Pakistan, and Canada, pledged to help repel Hussein's troops unless they withdrew; the UN set a January 1991 deadline for that withdrawal. Hussein responded by attacking nearby Israel with scud missiles and detonating Kuwaiti oil wells instead.

On January 17, 1991, Operation Desert Storm commenced with the bombing of Iraqi troops inside Kuwait; a ground assault began a month later, on February 23, and after fewer than 100 hours Kuwait had been liberated. Soon after, British, French, and American troops moved to within 150 miles (240km) of the capital city of Baghdad but were ordered to withdraw to the Kuwaiti border.

Faltering Economy, Political Reality

While the Gulf War had been successful, millions of Americans found themselves out of work. Between 1990 and 1992, the unemployment rate spiked from 5.3 percent to 7.5 percent. The big three US car manufacturers—Ford, Chrysler, and General Motors—lost more than $5 billion in 1991 alone, and computer giant IBM laid off 60,000 workers. Suddenly average workers were wondering what had happened to the American dream of being able to buy a house and make better lives for themselves and their families.

On the eve of the 1992 elections, Bush's popularity appeared more fragile than ever. Politically, the time seemed right for a new direction. Into this arena came a dark horse, a politician from a tiny, southern state who, on paper, looked unlikely to carry an election.

William Jefferson Clinton had grown up poor in Hope, Arkansas. His traveling salesman father died in a car accident three months before Bill was born on August 19, 1946. His mother Virginia put her baby

Diana: The People's Princess

O ne of the world's most famous faces of the 1990s was that of Diana Spencer, a shy young woman who married Prince Charles, heir to the British throne. Their grand wedding in 1981 at St. Paul's Cathedral in London was televised around the world and watched by more than 750 million people. The marriage produced two sons, Princes William and Harry, but was otherwise fraught with infidelity and mistrust. Still, over the course of 15 years, Diana remained a popular figure within the royal family as she supported charitable causes around the world, including AIDS research. After the couple divorced in 1996, Diana worked to eradicate land mines that maimed and killed thousands of people each year.

By early 1997 Diana had found love again with Dodi Fayed, the son of a wealthy London merchant. The media seemed obsessed with Diana, and on the night of August 31, 2007, Diana and Fayed's limousine sped away from their Paris hotel to escape the flashbulbs of photographers. Moments later, the vehicle crashed in a tunnel. Diana, Fayed, and their driver Henri Paul were killed. British and French investigators later concluded that Paul was likely intoxicated and driving recklessly at the time of the accident. On September 6 Diana's sons walked behind the gun carriage that bore the coffin of their mother. Hundreds of thousands of mourners lined the streets as the procession made its way to Westminster Abbey for the funeral. When asked whether Diana had found a new way to be royal, Prime Minister Tony Blair said no. Instead, he said, "Diana taught us a new way to be British."

Quoted in Catherine Mayer, "How Diana Transformed Britain," *Time*, August 16, 2007. www. time.com.

in the care of her parents while she attended nursing school. From his humble roots, Clinton rose to the Arkansas governorship in 1979, and in 1992 he threw his hat into the presidential ring. With his wife Hillary, Clinton challenged the Republican political machine, which had helped elect five Republican candidates in the previous six presidential elections. A canny politician, Clinton determined to make the election about the economy. His campaign's unofficial slogan, "It's the economy, stupid!" galvanized audiences across the nation.

To push his message, Clinton undermined Bush's presidential image by portraying the wealthy elder statesman as out of touch with average Americans. During one televised debate, Clinton scored with audiences because he knew the price of a loaf of bread and Bush did not.

A New President

Despite the best Republican efforts, the charismatic, youthful, and saxophone-playing Democrat could not be stopped. On Election Day, Clinton won only 43 percent of the popular vote to Bush's 37.5 percent, but his electoral college victory was a landslide 370 votes to 168. Along with his vice president Al Gore, Clinton determined to make good on the promises he had campaigned on. But one of his first initiatives—to provide all Americans with affordable health care—met harsh resistance.

To get the health care legislation through Congress the president enlisted his wife Hillary Rodham Clinton. But the First Lady, an accomplished attorney, rubbed many lawmakers and average citizens the wrong way. Although the Clinton plan included keeping health care costs low by promoting competition among providers, powerful lobbyists for the insurance industry fought the plan and aired television commercials casting doubt on whether average citizens would be able to retain their health coverage under a new law. By 1994 polls strongly suggested that most Americans were not in favor of changes in their health care.

Soon after, the president gave up on his dream of universal health care. This failure and others ushered in a Republican takeover of Congress in 1994 led by Georgia congressman Newt Gingrich, who became Speaker of the House. He and his fellow Republicans consequently drew up their own plan for American renewal called the "Contract with America." The contract included promises to pass a balanced budget amendment, limit judicial appeals for criminals, and enact strict welfare reform. The passage of these and other laws seemed to suggest long-term Republican control of Congress and dark days for the Clinton administration.

War and Genocide

While Clinton battled at home trying to pass his agenda, the world's attention had turned to Eastern Europe. With the end of Soviet communism in the late 1980s, former states once controlled by the USSR began breaking away or simply dissolved. Yugoslavia, one of the largest areas, included a number of republics or provinces. As the separate states began declaring independence, desire for control only deepened the crisis.

In Kosovo, a small region once part of the former Yugoslavia, paramilitary forces from Serbia, a neighboring state, were perpetrating acts of ethnic cleansing—murder based on cultural background—against Albanian Muslims. Serb militias, often consisting of village locals, typically rounded up Albanian men and boys, loaded them into trucks, drove them into the surrounding mountains, and then shot them to death.

Hundreds of thousands of Albanians tried to escape. Humanitarian organizations opened medical relief camps to treat more than 300,000 refugees who made it across the border to Macedonia. In March 1999, the North Atlantic Treaty Organization (NATO), an alliance of democratic states in Europe and North America, began bombing targets in the former Yugoslavia as a way of driving the Serbs out of Kosovo and stemming the violence.

The central African nation of Rwanda also devolved into mass murder during the decade. After the country's president died in a mysterious plane crash in April 1994, influential members of his Hutu tribe blamed a rival tribe, the Tutsis, for his death. Soon, lawless bands of Hutu militia began hacking Tutsi men, women, and children to death with machetes.

Over the course of 100 days these armed forces killed over 800,000 people. A UN force stationed in Rwanda refused to become involved and failed to halt the killing because UN policy stipulated that its forces could not intervene unless fired upon. After the horror, many survivors constructed makeshift memorials to the dead, in many cases leaving the bones of Rwanda's victims where they lay.

The Rise of Religious Extremism

Like the murderers in Rwanda and the former Yugoslavia, religious extremists from the Middle East proved ruthless in their desire to destroy their enemies. On February 26, 1993, a group of Islamic terrorists led by Kuwaiti Ramzi Yousef detonated a truck bomb below the North Tower of the World Trade Center in New York City. Although the plot failed in its attempt to bring down the towers, the explosion and smoke killed six people and injured 1,042 more. At his trial, Yousef admitted his role in the bombing and pledged to continue fighting what he called American terrorism around the world.

Like Yousef, Saudi-born millionaire Osama bin Laden despised the United States and its close ally Israel. In August 1996, five years after the Gulf War, Bin Laden, who had been financially supporting Muslim extremists for years, declared war on the United States. Much of his anger toward the United States stemmed from the nation's continued post–Gulf War presence in his homeland Saudi Arabia. Although the Saudis welcomed the American presence, Bin Laden saw the US troops as an insult to Islam. "Terrorizing you, while you are carrying arms in our land, is a legitimate right and a moral obligation,"[6] said Bin Laden in a videotaped statement broadcast around the world.

Three years later, Bin Laden and his terrorist organization, known as al Qaeda, threatened all-out warfare on the United States. But according to author Lawrence Wright, few members of American intelligence organizations, including the CIA, took Bin Laden's threat, or al Qaeda, seriously. "Up against the confidence that Americans placed in modernity and technology . . . the defiant gestures of bin Laden and his followers seemed absurd and even pathetic,"[7] says Wright.

By 1996 US intelligence services learned that Bin Laden was devising a plot to assassinate Clinton. Although that never came to pass,

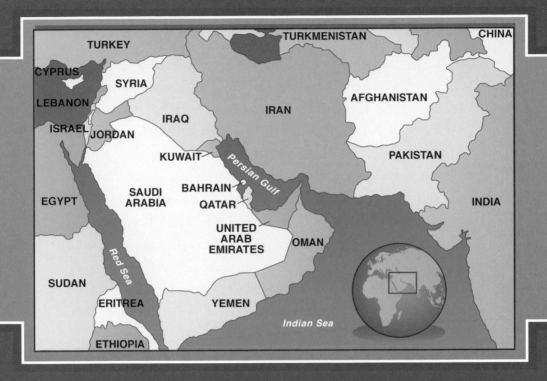

two other al Qaeda plots did. On August 7, 1998, operatives detonated truck bombs at US embassies in the East African nations of Kenya and Tanzania, killing nearly 300 people. Bin Laden's terrorist organization was growing stronger and more potent than ever.

American Extremism

While global extremism grew, an American version was also bubbling to the surface. In February 1993, federal agents executed a warrant on the Branch Davidian ranch in Waco, Texas. The Branch Davidians were a religious sect led by self-proclaimed prophet David Koresh. Former members of the group and criminal investigators alleged that children were being sexually abused within the group's large, heavily

Columbine Tragedy

The morning of April 20, 1999, started normally at Colorado's Columbine High School. But at 11 a.m. two students, Eric Harris and Dylan Klebold, carried one duffel bag into the school cafeteria and another into the kitchen. Both contained homemade propane tank bombs. Outside, the pair, now armed with a pistol, rifle, and two sawed-off shotguns, waited for the bombs to explode. They did not explode. Harris and Klebold moved to the school's west entrance and at 11:19 began shooting. Firing at will and tossing pipe bombs as they moved inside the building, the two eventually entered the school library where 52 people cowered in fear. Harris asked all people wearing white hats to stand. When no one did, Harris and Klebold walked from table to table shooting some and sparing others until 11:42 when they exited the library and wandered the school hallways. Thirteen people were dead and 24 wounded.

By now, SWAT teams had gathered on the school grounds, helping injured students to safety and hoping to take down the killers. When they entered the school they found Harris and Klebold dead of self-inflicted gunshots. In the days and weeks after Columbine, the fourth deadliest school massacre in US history, investigators theorized that bullying or video games or drugs had driven the two students to commit their heinous act. In time, though, these explanations were disproved. Instead, says psychologist Peter Langman, "These are not ordinary kids who were bullied into retaliation. . . . These arc kids with serious psychological problems."

Quoted in Greg Toppo, "10 Years Later, the Real Story Behind Columbine," *USA Today*, April 4, 2009. www.usatoday.com.

guarded compound. Authorities also believed that Koresh and his followers were stockpiling guns.

These concerns were borne out when federal agents attempted to serve their search warrant: A two-hour gun battle between officers from the Bureau of Alcohol, Tobacco, Firearms, and Explosives (ATF) and sect members left four agents and six Branch Davidian members dead. The incident was followed by a 50-day stalemate, after which the FBI began a new assault in April 19, 1993. They pumped tear gas into the main building, but another firefight ensued. Shortly thereafter, the building caught on fire. Seventy-six people, including 20 children and leader David Koresh, died.

During the 50-day standoff, former US Army soldier Timothy McVeigh drove to Waco to show his support for the Branch Davidians. He spoke to reporters about what he believed was the government's desire to curb gun rights. "Once you take away the guns," he said, "you can do anything to the people. . . . The government is continually growing bigger and more powerful and the people need to prepare to defend themselves against government control."[8] McVeigh was part of an ever-growing, loosely organized movement to overthrow the federal government. He found some sympathizers during the next few months as he traveled to gun shows across the United States.

In early 1995 McVeigh and an old army buddy, Terry Nichols, built an explosive by mixing 5,000 pounds of ammonium nitrate and nitromethane, a fuel used in motor racing. They placed their device in the back of a Ryder moving truck. On the morning of April 19, 1995—the anniversary of the Waco tragedy—McVeigh drove it to the front of the Alfred P. Murrah Federal Building in Oklahoma City, Oklahoma. After lighting a five-minute fuse, he parked the truck and walked away. At 9:02 a.m. the truck exploded, shattering the facade of the Murrah Building and destroying the day care center housed on its second floor. The blast killed 168 people, 19 of whom were small children.

Captured soon after, McVeigh showed little, if any, remorse. In 1997 a jury found McVeigh guilty on all 11 federal counts against him. He was executed by lethal injection in 2001. Accomplice Terry Nichols was convicted for his role and sentenced to life in prison.

Economy and the Internet

By the year of McVeigh's execution, the shaky US economy of the early 1990s had disappeared, replaced by a growing one. Nationwide unemployment stood at only 4.8 percent, and the job market exploded. This helped Clinton's popularity among Americans, which soared to 60 percent. National debt and the budget deficit dwindled as tax revenue increased. In 1997 the budget deficit stood at $25 billion, lower than at any time since 1974. The economic horizon promised even better news: 1998 was expected to bring a federal budget surplus in the billions of dollars. Wall Street also boomed, and Americans envisioned a future of financial prosperity and security.

Part of the reason behind this breathtaking economic upswing was the evolution and development of the Internet. Once used as a communication tool among university students, the World Wide Web had broken through to the general public in the early 1990s and now seemed poised to revolutionize the way people around the world communicated and retrieved information. The development of web browsers such as Netscape and Mosaic made it easier for the general public to use the Internet. And use it they did: In 1996, 18 million people were "surfing" the Internet. One year later, 30 million adults had logged on, and by 1998, 20 percent of all American households had an Internet connection.

The popularity of the web was coupled with success in Internet businesses such as America Online (AOL). In its early years, AOL served 30 percent of all Internet users in the United States, but other companies quickly began competing for the millions of people now demanding Internet services and destinations. Amazon.com, founded by Jeff Bezos in the late 1990s, began selling books online but soon began selling all sorts of products that consumers traditionally purchased at "brick and mortar" stores.

This new wave of companies also began trading stock, and millions of people invested in businesses they were certain could earn them money. Web company employees, many of whom accepted stock options as part of their compensation, often became millionaires overnight when investors propelled a company's stock into the stratosphere. American

The 1990s saw the development of homegrown extremism in the form of Timothy McVeigh. McVeigh expressed his antigovernment views by blowing up the Alfred P. Murrah Federal Building in Oklahoma City, killing 168 people. Heavy equipment is used to clear debris a week after the deadly blast.

economic growth—jobs and government revenue, especially—became more and more tied to the success of the Internet in the late 1990s, but many experts feared that such extraordinary web growth could not last.

Impeachment

Despite the Wall Street doubters, by 1997 the strong economic outlook enhanced Clinton's popularity among average Americans—but not among his Republican rivals on Capitol Hill. Open warfare between the president and his more conservative opponents had loomed over the executive branch of government since Clinton took office. That warfare culminated in his 1998 impeachment, the first against a sitting US president in 130 years.

The impeachment came about after Kenneth Starr was named as the independent counsel and began investigating various accusations against Clinton. These included a real estate venture dating back to the president's time as Arkansas governor; the firing of staff members from the White House travel office; and sexual harassment allegations against Clinton. During lengthy investigations, Starr was given tapes of intimate, record-ed conversations of Clinton talking on the telephone to White House intern Monica Lewinsky. Forced by a judge to testify soon after, Clin-ton denied any improper relationship with Lewinsky. Starr, meanwhile, believed he had evidence that the president was lying. In January 1998 Clinton publicly denied an affair with Lewinsky. Months later Clinton admitted that his relations with Lewinsky were improper.

The US House of Representatives took up the matter of his lying in testimony after the November 1998 midterm elections. Many Repub-licans encouraged Clinton to resign. On December 19, 1998, Clinton was impeached by a vote of 228-206—the first American president to be impeached since Andrew Johnson in 1868. The subsequent Senate trial lasted more than a month. Sixty-seven votes—two-thirds of the Senate—were needed to remove the president from office, but Repub-licans could only muster 45 votes on charges of perjury, or lying while under oath, and 50 votes on charges of obstruction of justice.

As Clinton's term in office drew to a close in late 2000, Americans began to question the kinds of qualities that their next president should have. For millions of them, this meant not only electing a competent leader but a moral one. Clinton's relationship with a White House in-tern and his subsequent denial of that relationship had convinced many that the country needed to move in a new, scandal-free direction.

Beginning and Ending

As the final decade of the twentieth century dimmed, the world appeared on the precipice of a new wave of prosperity. Global financial markets were booming, debt was low, and war had, for the most part, receded. Many world leaders promised a twenty-first century transformation—one that would serve the suffering masses and usher in an era of lasting peace. Only time would tell whether that promise would be kept.

Chapter 2

Politics, War, and Terrorism

The 2000s began ominously as news outlets around the world warned of a computer glitch that could cause software to fail on an epic scale once the new decade dawned. This Y2K scare—caused by programmers who for years had abbreviated the year with two digits rather than four—made headlines on an almost daily basis as the year 2000 approached. Global predictions of cyber doom did not come to pass. On the horizon, though, a millennial election loomed in the United States. Its result would have dramatic consequences in the young century.

Election 2000

The first presidential election of the new decade promised a referendum on the Clinton years. Bill Clinton's vice president Al Gore hoped to succeed his boss, and as the campaign for president began in 1999, Gore decided to distance himself from the chief executive and the scandals of his administration.

Gore's Republican opponent, Texas governor George W. Bush, eldest son of former president George H.W. Bush, cultivated a homespun charm and a folksy charisma. When Americans went to the polls on Election Day, the voting reflected the conflicted American psyche. Americans were happy with the nation's economic strides. Many had good jobs, their wages were rising, and a smaller budget deficit meant that the United States could remain debt free and financially competitive with other nations for years to come. Others were so disgusted by Bill Clinton's personal behavior that they were determined to move in a different political direction. The choice between the presidential candidates was stark: Gore, professorial and awkward, Bush unpolished but likeable.

As election night wore on, television news commentators were unable to announce a winner, although Gore appeared to be leading Bush in the popular vote by 500,000. But as Americans awoke the next morning, the identity of their future leader remained a mystery. Florida and its 27 electoral votes had become the make-or-break state. Six million votes had been cast there; Bush led by approximately 1,700 votes. This slim margin became even slimmer when a required machine recount put the difference between the two candidates at 500, with Bush still ahead.

Investigators found irregularities in Sunshine State voting, particularly in the paper ballots that voters had to manually punch holes in to cast a ballot. The remaining paper fragments, or "chads," became a point of contention as the hand recounts began since officials could not always be certain which canidate voters meant to cast a ballot for. For 36 days the country waited to find out who would be the next president. Attorneys for Bush and Gore kept a close watch on the recounts and used whatever legal avenues they could: Bush's lawyers wanted the recounts to stop, fearing that Gore might overtake their client; Gore's lawyers petitioned to keep the recounts going.

The election madness ended on December 12—the day that Florida had to certify a winner—when the US Supreme Court handed down a final ruling: In a 5-4 decision, the justices said that since the recounts could not be completed by the deadline, Florida had to cease its recounting and recertify George W. Bush as the new president-elect of the United States. In his dissenting opinion, Justice John Paul Stevens made his disdain for the verdict clear: "Although we may never know with complete certainty the identity of the winner of this year's Presidential election, the identity of the loser is perfectly clear. It is the Nation's confidence in the judge as an impartial guardian of the rule of law."[9]

9/11 Terrorist Attacks

During the spring and summer months of Bush's first year in office in 2001, intelligence agents began warning of looming terrorist threats. The warnings went unheeded, and on September 11, 2001, at 8:46 a.m. Eastern

"Mission Accomplished"

On May 1, 2003, less than two months after American military forces invaded Iraq, President George W. Bush became the first sitting president to land in a fixed-wing aircraft—a Lockheed S-3 Viking—on an aircraft carrier. His presence on the USS *Abraham Lincoln* was to announce the end of major combat operations in Iraq. After landing, Bush stood in his flight suit and posed for photographs with navy personnel. Later that day he spoke to the nation in a speech carried around the world over television and the Internet. To cheering men and women in uniform, the president spoke of victory in toppling Iraq's brutal dictator, Saddam Hussein. Behind him hung a banner with the words "Mission Accomplished" printed on a field of stars and stripes.

Over the next several years, Iraq fell into great turmoil, as warring factions and terrorist groups disrupted the US mission to stabilize the country, killing thousands of Iraqis and American soldiers. For critics of the war, the banner became a symbol of what they saw as the arrogance and incompetence of the Bush administration. During his final press conference before leaving office on January 12, 2009, the president appeared to acknowledge his blunder: "Clearly, putting a 'Mission Accomplished' on an aircraft carrier was a mistake. It sent the wrong message."

Quoted in Sheryl Gay Stolberg, "Mistakes, I've Made a Few, Bush Tells Reporters," *New York Times*, January 12, 2009. www.nytimes.com.

Standard Time (EST), American Airlines Flight 11 crashed into the North Tower of the World Trade Center, one of the two tallest buildings in New York City. Initial television reports of the event puzzled many Americans.

It appeared to be little more than a terrible accident. For more than 15 minutes, news commentators worked frantically to find out more information about what had happened. At 9:03 a.m., as millions watched, another airplane—United Airlines Flight 175—barreled into the South Tower of the World Trade Center. What may at first have seemed like a terrible accident now appeared to be an act of terrorism. Enormous plumes of smoke billowed from the crippled Twin Towers. The nation's largest city was under siege.

First responders raced to the scene, but six stairwells were instantly cut off by the impact. Thousands worked in the towers, and many working on the floors above where the airplanes hit found it impossible to escape. In desperation, dozens, perhaps hundreds, of people trapped in these upper floors leaped 1,728 feet (527m) to their deaths. Many of those working on the lower floors tried to find escape routes, often

An army helicopter flies over the Pentagon after an airliner hijacked by terrorists crashed into the building on September 11, 2001. A total of 125 people, both aboard the plane and in the building, died.

passing firefighters and police who were rushing to the upper floors to save those in need.

The scalding fires that broke out in the wake of the crashed jetliners quickly melted the buildings' internal trusses that held the floors and walls together. These trusses were no match for the intense heat generated and fed by leaking jet fuel fires. Fifty-six minutes after it had been attacked, the South Tower fell; 102 minutes after it had been struck, the North Tower followed. Smoke and debris from the fallen buildings created a massive cloud of dust that bathed the city in gray smog for days.

Lost Lives, Lost Opportunities

Of the 2,759 people who had lost their lives in the Twin Towers, 10 were hijackers and 157 were airline passengers and crew members on the doomed airplanes. Of the 406 first responders who also perished, 343 were members of the Fire Department of New York. Flight 93, a hijacked plane aimed at the US Capitol, was brought down when passengers attempted to commandeer the plane. It crashed in a Pennsylvania field, killing 44 people. A fourth and final plane crashed into the Pentagon, killing 125 people on the plane and in the fortified building.

In July 2004 the 9/11 Commission released its findings on the tragedy after two years of investigations. The report criticized the federal government and intelligence agencies for not recognizing the seriousness of the threat earlier. The commission uncovered strong evidence that al Qaeda terrorists had spent months planning the attack and that at a least one had enrolled in an American flight school to learn how to fly—but not land—a plane. The report concluded that few could have imagined that the terrorists would try to hijack so many planes at the same time. It called this lack of forethought a "failure of imagination."[10]

War on Terror

With a nation in shock and deeply grieving, Bush stood before a joint session of Congress on September 20, 2001, and promised retribution, a "War on Terror": "Tonight, we are a country awakened to danger and called to defend freedom. Our grief has turned to anger and anger

The 2000s proved fateful to the Israeli-Palestinian conflict, which had raged for decades. The two sides came close to a peace accord at the Camp David summit in July 2000, but negotiations broke down. In late September 2000, former Israeli general Ariel Sharon enraged Palestinians with his visit to the Haram al Sharif, or Noble Sanctuary, in Jerusalem. Palestinian Muslims consider the site the third holiest place in Islam; they viewed Sharon's visit as an insult and a provocation. The following day dozens of them stood near the sanctuary and hurled stones at Jews praying at the Western Wall, a site that is sacred to Jews. Israeli troops responded with gunfire that killed seven. Riots erupted soon after, and the second intifada, or "uprising," had begun. (An earlier uprising, known as the first intifada, had lasted from 1987 to 1993.)

Within days, Israeli soldiers and Palestinian demonstrators began firing at one another in Jerusalem. A 12-year-old Palestinian boy was caught in the cross fire and killed. The child's death only fueled Palestinian anger. A few weeks later, Israeli outrage peaked as well when two Israeli soldiers were detained in the Palestinian town of Ramallah. A vicious mob broke into police headquarters where the soldiers were being held and killed them. The violence had quickly gone from bad to worse, and it continued until 2005, when the second intifada finally came to an end. In nearly five years, 6,500 Palestinians and 1,100 Israelis had died.

to resolution. Whether we bring our enemies to justice or bring justice to our enemies, justice will be done."[11] Bush took care to blame the terrorist attacks not on Islam but on extremists who called themselves Muslims yet distorted the religion's teachings.

The Bush administration responded to the 9/11 attacks by invading Afghanistan on October 7, 2001. Afghanistan and its brutal regime, the Taliban, had harbored Osama bin Laden and other al Qaeda leaders during the buildup to the attacks. The war began as an effort to demolish the terrorist organization and bring its leadership to justice. Working in tandem with the Afghani group Northern Alliance, sworn enemies of the Taliban, US forces quickly ran the Taliban off.

Harder to defeat, though, was Bin Laden himself. He remained at large and bragged about the attacks. In December American forces and their allies obtained evidence that suggested Bin Laden was hiding in the Tora Bora Mountains, along Afghanistan's border with Pakistan. The Americans won the fierce battle that ensued, but Bin Laden somehow escaped.

Thus, suggests journalist Ahmed Rashid, the overall victory remained incomplete. "The failure of the USA to destroy Al Qaeda and the Afghan Taliban leadership in the 2001 war allowed many Taliban and Al Qaeda commanders and fighters to escape into Pakistan and take up safe residence."[12]

Iraq

The failure to eliminate the terrorist leadership and stabilize Afghanistan was largely the result of a new American target in the War on Terrorism: Iraq. In 2001 and 2002, the Bush administration began drawing connections between al Qaeda and Saddam Hussein's Iraqi Intelligence Service. The president himself said that Hussein and al Qaeda "work in concert" and that Iraq "has longstanding and continuing ties to terrorist organizations, and there are [al Qaeda] terrorists inside Iraq."[13] In the months and years that followed, the alleged ties between Hussein's despotic but secular regime and the religiously extremist Bin Laden–run terror network could never be proved, but that mattered little in the winter of 2003.

The invasion of Iraq, known as Operation Iraqi Freedom, began on March 20 of that year. The immediate goal was to subdue Hussein's regime and seek out the nuclear and chemical weapons (called weapons of mass destruction or WMD) that the Bush administration was certain existed. American forces promised a "shock and awe" campaign carried out with precision missile strikes in and around the Iraqi capital of Baghdad. For 20 days, by land and by air, American armed forces battled a weak but persistent Iraqi army, including Hussein's elite Republican Guard. On the twenty-first day of combat missions, American troops entered the smoldering city of Baghdad.

Many Iraqis took to the streets to celebrate, even toppling a statue of Hussein. But from the successful first phase of the conflict emerged a darker and more drawn out postwar period, as the jubilation of Iraqis quickly turned into chaos. Looting and general unrest swept the country, and American soldiers, who had been given little instruction on how to deal with the aftermath of the invasion, could do little to stop it.

Terror on a Global Scale

Terrorism and unrest in other parts of the world continued as well, as al Qaeda and various extremist groups persisted in their attempts to disrupt and destroy the lives of innocent civilians. Although overshadowed by the 9/11 tragedy, three other terrorist acts put nations on notice that terrorism had to be confronted.

The first occurred in Madrid, Spain, on the morning of March 11, 2004, when a terrorist cell exploded 10 coordinated bombs on four commuter trains. The rush hour bombings killed 191 people and injured nearly 1,800. Occurring three days before Spain's general elections, warring political parties quickly blamed one another for distorting or hiding information about the terrorist plot. In those elections, incumbent Spanish prime minister José María Aznar of the Partido Popular Party was defeated. Analysts suggested that had Aznar and his party handled the aftermath of the bombing better he might have retained his elected office. Later, the Spanish judiciary tied the tragedy to an al Qaeda–inspired terrorist group.

London, too, became a target on July 7, 2005, when al Qaeda–affiliated operatives set off four bombs. Three were detonated on three

Terror and Conflict in the 2000s

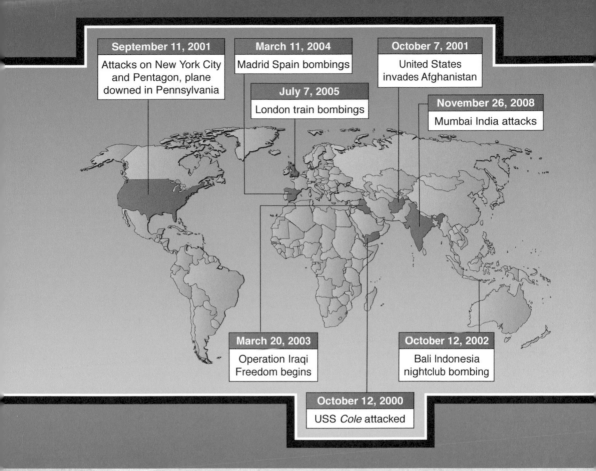

September 11, 2001
Attacks on New York City and Pentagon, plane downed in Pennsylvania

March 11, 2004
Madrid Spain bombings

October 7, 2001
United States invades Afghanistan

July 7, 2005
London train bombings

November 26, 2008
Mumbai India attacks

March 20, 2003
Operation Iraqi Freedom begins

October 12, 2002
Bali Indonesia nightclub bombing

October 12, 2000
USS *Cole* attacked

of the city's subway trains; the fourth was exploded on a double-decker bus in London's Tavistock Square. Fifty-two Londoners were killed; 700 were injured. Each of the homemade devices were stuffed into backpacks and carried to their targets by young men inspired by the philosophy of Bin Laden. Three of the four were of Pakistani descent.

In videotapes made before their suicide missions, the terrorists spoke of their opposition to Great Britain's involvement in the Iraq War and its support of Saudi Arabia. "Your democratically elected governments continuously perpetuate atrocities against my people all over the world," said 30-year-old bomber Mohammad Sidique Khan in his final statement. "And your support of them makes you directly responsible, just as I am directly responsible for protecting and avenging my Muslim brothers and sisters."[14]

Another deadly post–9/11 attack occurred on November 26, 2008, in Mumbai, India. On that day, 10 men from a Pakistan-based terror organization called Lashkar-e-Taiba arrived in the city on speedboats. The terrorists then targeted local hotels, holding hundreds hostage and going on a three-day shooting spree that killed 166 people and injured 300. One British tourist's ordeal was typical. She spent six hours barricaded in the Oberoi Hotel, fearing that if she tried to escape she would be shot. "There were about 20 or 30 people in each room," she said. "The doors were locked very quickly, the lights turned off, and everybody just lay very still on the floor."[15]

More than ever, citizens around the world had to be on guard against unattended suitcases and packages and strange behavior at airports. While no remedy was foolproof, people worked to minimize threats of death and mass destruction.

Nuclear Threat: North Korea

The twenty-first century brought a fear of deadly terrorist groups such as al Qaeda. But, according to many of the world's leaders, the isolated nation of North Korea posed an equally dangerous threat. The secretive nature of the country's leaders and its refusal to join the community of nations in peace treaties and other pacts worried many heads of state around the globe and in Asia specifically.

Korea had been separated into two independent nations in 1945; war followed until 1953. Since then, tensions between democratic South Korea and autocratic North Korea only festered. By the twenty-first century, North Korea, led by unpredictable dictator Kim Jong Il, had acquired a small but potent arsenal of nuclear missiles.

Over the course of the decade, North Korea's government starved its people, ruled them with an iron fist, and bragged about its ability to inflict devastating war if challenged. The country's No Dong missiles, by 2005, had a range of 870 miles (1,400km), enough to inflict damage on South Korea, Japan, and parts of China and Russia. Missile tests during the decade sometimes succeeded and often failed, but Kim Jong Il's desire to play diplomatic cat and mouse left much of Asia on edge.

After UN sanctions were imposed in June 2009, North Korea again tested a series of missiles in the Sea of Japan in a clear attempt to prove its might. Citizens of South Korea, the most likely target in any attack, remained frustrated. "We sent them food, fertilizer, factories, more than we give our own poor people," says South Korean Lee Soon-hwan. "And all they pay us back with is this nuclear test."[16]

Bush vs. Kerry

For most of the decade, South Korea's most reliable ally, the United States, remained in the midst of two costly wars. By 2004 the tepid economy in the United States also appeared to make Bush's reelection bid a challenge. Although he enjoyed great popularity after the 9/11

Rescue workers cover bodies following the March 2004 rush hour bombing of passenger trains in Madrid, Spain. Extremism and terror touched many countries during the decade of the 2000s.

attacks, many Americans had soured on the president after the fall of Baghdad and the chaos that followed. Bush's Democratic challenger for the presidency, Massachusetts senator John Kerry, was a decorated veteran of the Vietnam War. Kerry saw the Iraq War as a disastrous mistake that was putting the lives of soldiers and innocent Iraqi civilians in harm's way and bankrupting the nation.

On Election Day, Americans went to the polls hoping either to reelect a president they viewed as a principled and steady leader or toss out a president they saw as incompetent and dangerous. In the end, Bush carried 31 of 50 states, receiving a total of 286 electoral votes. The popular vote was far closer, with Bush getting 50.7 percent and Kerry earning 48.3 percent. In addition to Bush's triumph, the GOP also swept the House of Representatives and the Senate. The Republican victory was complete and total for the first time since 1928.

In the days after his reelection, Bush promised to reform the Social Security system and make prescription drugs cheaper for the elderly. But the president's domestic agenda would remain largely sidetracked by the worsening situation in Iraq. Former dictator Saddam Hussein had been captured in December 2003. Three years later, on December 30, 2006, he was tried on charges of murder and torture and executed for those crimes. By this time, Iraq had descended into chaos, as factions of Shiite and Sunni Muslims made war on one another.

The United States had little success in curbing the horrendous violence in Iraq during the decade. Looming even larger were the ongoing threats posed by terrorist groups that vowed to strike anywhere and at any time. On a daily basis, leaders from Mumbai to Sydney to Moscow grappled with the possibility of devastating attacks and worked to secure their cities and airports.

Chapter 3

Science, Technology, and the Power of Nature

Nineteenth- and twentieth-century science-fiction writers had long imagined the world at the turn of the twenty-first century. From glass skyscrapers that reached high into the clouds to flying cars to mind control and cloning, these predictions fascinated and excited readers in their day. Perhaps most famously, Arthur C. Clarke's 1968 novel *2001: A Space Odyssey* looked closely at the dangers of technology. In one chilling passage, a spaceship is commandeered by the HAL 9000 computer, which kills one astronaut and compels another to abandon the spacecraft. The new millennium did not bring the takeover of humans by technology, but it did witness scientific breakthroughs and transformations in the way people communicate.

Genomes and Stem Cells

The future came to pass in 2000, when scientists from the National Institutes of Health (NIH), along with experts from India, China, Japan, Germany, France, and Great Britain made a stunning announcement: After 10 years and at a cost of $3 billion, they had successfully created a working draft of the human genome, the sequence of chemical pairs that make up human DNA. Scientists believed that determining the precise sequence could help people better understand some of the key processes of the human body, including illness, aging, and death.

The idea for electronic books, or e-books, came about in the early 1970s but was not feasible until the Internet revolution of the 1990s. The idea is a simple one: Choose a book title from an online store; download the title; and read it on a smaller, book-sized version of a computer screen. The first e-book readers were launched in 1998 but failed to catch on.

E-readers finally clicked in the decade of the 2000s. Microsoft developed its reader in 2000 and Sony brought its version onto the market in 2006. As download speeds increased, more book lovers purchased e-book readers, but not until November 2007 and the introduction of Amazon's Kindle did the demand for e-books begin to explode. The e-book marked a dramatic but relatively small shift away from bound, hard copy books. Those who use e-book readers enjoy the ability to enlarge type, store thousands of books electronically, and purchase their reading material from home. The phenomenon is showing no signs of abating. By July 2010 Amazon announced that it was selling 143 e-books for every 100 hardcover books. A new book revolution had begun.

With the working draft completed, the NIH raced to complete the sequencing itself. But the institute faced competition from Celera Corporation, a private firm conducting a parallel project. Both organizations released the fully mapped human genome sequence in 2003. While the scientific potential for using the genome appeared limitless, experts remained unsure about how to use it. "The completion of the Human Genome Project in 2003 provided a general map of the DNA sequences of the human genome," write scholars Alison Bashford and Philippa Levine, but "we still do not know how far it is possible to develop practical methods in this direction."[17]

A scientific breakthrough with more immediate but controversial applications was stem cell research. Humans, like all multicellular organisms, have molecular cells that can renew themselves. By the dawn of the twenty-first century, scientists around the world were working with these human stem cells in laboratories in the hope that the microscopic matter might help doctors treat or even cure debilitating diseases such as Alzheimer's and Parkinson's.

One type of stem cell—considered by many scientists to be the most promising type for disease research—is found in the human embryo, a cluster of cells that become a fetus eight weeks after conception. But to carry out experiments and tests, lab workers must destroy the embryo. Detractors believed that destroying embryos amounted to a form of abortion. In many developed countries few regulations existed to stop such scientific work. In fact, in many places, governments funded the research. But in the summer of 2001 the stem cell controversy became heated in the United States. Proponents countered pro-life activists by arguing that federal funding was essential to any future progress.

On August 9, 2001, George W. Bush spoke to the nation from his home in Crawford, Texas, in a televised speech. He initially framed the argument in religious terms and spoke of the moral implications of his decision. He acknowledged the privately funded use of 60 stem cell lines but denied future federal funding for the research.

Music Revolution

Like stem cell research, music technology also came of age in the new millennium. Downloading favorite tunes from computer websites rather than buying traditional CDs began among high school and college students in the late 1990s. By 2001 a quarter of a billion songs were estimated to have been downloaded, most of them illegally.

According to music journalist Hank Bordowitz, "The record companies' worst nightmares were coming true: chased by the interconnected monster of the Internet, they jumped off a cliff of revenues and kept falling and falling, only they didn't wake up."[18]

The nightmares abated in 2001 with the advent of the Apple iPod. Housed in a small plastic case but able to store thousands of MP3 files, the iPod was stylish, colorful, and easy to use. Consumers could legally purchase the music they loved from an online iTunes store for 99 cents per song. By the fall of 2009, 220 million iPods had been sold worldwide.

Soon, iPod imitators were flooding the market; MP3 features were added to all new cars; and digital, portable music files became the standard method of music distribution. In 2005 digital music accounted for 6 percent of all music sales. By the end of the decade that percentage had increased dramatically to 40 percent.

Colonies of human embryonic stem cells are placed under a microscope for viewing. By the dawn of the twenty-first century, scientists worldwide were conducting stem cell research in hopes of someday curing Alzheimer's and Parkinson's diseases among others.

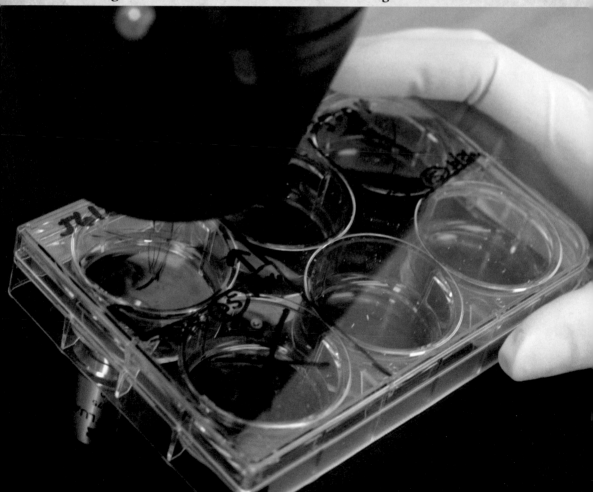

Cellular Celebration

The 2000s brought an equally startling change to telephone communication. Continuous innovation transformed large, clunky phones into sleek, small devices the size of a candy bar. These devices were also capable of performing a wider variety of tasks than ever before, and by the end of the decade over 4 billion people throughout the world had them.

In 2000, Ericsson, a telecommunications company, introduced the R380, the world's first "smartphone," which enabled consumers to simply touch a small computer screen to work their device. One year later the first camera phone was introduced in Japan, and developments in speed and bandwidth made it possible for people to surf the Internet through their phones, something they once could only do from their computers.

Over the next 10 years, the concept of the smartphone evolved as companies such as Nokia, RIM, and Handspring added new features to their products as a way of attracting new customers. Then in 2007 Apple released the iPhone and changed the industry. It allowed users to tailor their device: By simply touching a screen and downloading one of millions of "apps," or applications, consumers could personalize their devices and stream videos, read the news, get advice on fashion, or find the nearest restaurant with the click of a button.

Before long, the personal app idea was built into other smartphones—the Curve and the Android among them—and became an industry standard. A new revolution in technology, says CBS journalist Brent Schendler, had begun: "We [consumers] are now witnessing the fastest evolution of a mass technology to date in what's also unmistakably the emergence of the next big genre of computing: the multipurpose, endlessly modifiable 'app phone.'"[19]

At virtually the same time, new forms of interaction, particularly texting and its message-posting offshoot Twitter, became popular with millions of people who felt just as comfortable using their fingers to type quick, informal notes to friends and family as talking to them. Such innovations in the way people connected and organized their lives changed the way the world lives, works, plays, and communicates.

TV, the Internet, and Newspapers

The twenty-first-century advent of smartphones and other handheld devices revolutionized the way people got their news and entertainment. With the click of a button, consumers hungry for information found all they needed. Consequently, this new technology meant that fewer people used more traditional media such as newspapers, magazines, and TV. Newspapers, especially, struggled to keep customers, as web-only media outlets sprung up, moving the hard copy version of the hometown newspaper toward obsolescence.

In 2009 alone, budget cutbacks and a weak economy caused 105 newspapers to close in the United States. Subsequently, 10,000 people lost their jobs, and advertising revenue fell by 30 percent. "Most of it [advertising] is simply being siphoned out of journalism altogether," writes business journalist Megan McArdle. "Craigslist ate the classified ads. eHarmony stole the personals. . . . And Macy's can email its own . . . customers to announce a sale."[20] The loss of advertising revenue hastened the demise of traditional news media outlets.

Television was also dramatically affected by the shifting media landscape. Network viewership had been down for decades, but now cable TV was suffering. Entertainment corporations such as Viacom and TimeWarner recognized that the only way they could remain competitive was to allow viewers to watch their favorite programs when it was convenient for them. By mid-decade, fans of popular television shows such as *Lost, Dexter*, or *The Bachelor* could now watch these programs on their own time by recording them with their digital video recorders (DVRs) and watching them later. Smartphones also became mini-TVs, too, as millions downloaded television shows, movies, and video clips from sites such as YouTube.

Where once consumers had to search for what they needed or remain at the mercy of TV executives and newspaper publishers, technology had severely threatened age-old industries. Companies soon realized that to remain competitive, they had to give people what they wanted when they wanted it. Consumers' unlimited access to any and all content forced providers to rethink the way they delivered their products.

Water on Mars

In June 2000, NASA scientists detected evidence of water on the planet Mars. Specifically, they traced and photographed what appeared to be an ancient valley, debris, and mud deposits that suggested the long-ago presence of flowing water. Researchers surmised that millennia ago, Mars may have contained deep oceans, and where water exists, life typically follows. What is less clear is whether water exists there today. NASA has yet to find water, but scientists suggest that may be because temperatures on Mars are well below zero, keeping any hidden water deposits frozen. Although the debate over the presence of water will no doubt continue, Michael Meyer, lead scientist for NASA's Mars Exploration Program, is excited about the continued exploration: "We've gone from suspecting there was water on Mars once upon a time to deciding there definitely was water, and not only that there was water, but lots of water. Now . . . the inventory of water on Mars is looking better and better as we learn more."

Quoted in Charles Q. Choi, "Water on Mars First Discovered 10 Years Ago. Is It Still There?," *Christian Science Monitor*, June 22, 2010. www.csmonitor.com.

"Googled"

Perhaps the first company to recognize the importance of putting digital content at peoples' fingertips was the Internet search engine Google, founded in 1998 by friends Sergey Brin and Larry Page. Google came of age in the 2000s, allowing anyone with a computer and an Internet connection to search the billions of websites across the globe for information. Google quickly became synonymous with "search"; the verb "google" became a catchword. By the late 2000s Google was running over 1 million servers to process the 1 billion search requests it received each day.

The demand for and popularity of Google also translated into huge profits. In 2006 alone, the company raked in $10 billion in advertising. "It fulfilled a need that millions of Internet users had yet to fully articulate," write business experts Rick Kash and David Calhoun. "Millions of people never knew they wanted Google . . . until they saw it."[21]

Enormous success also encouraged the company's founders to branch out. In 2005 they created Google Earth, a program that enables users to home in on any spot in the world with just a location and a click of a mouse, and Google Books, which provides free online access to millions of books and magazines. Google Translate, introduced in 2007, allows users to type in a phrase and have it translated it into one of dozens of languages, from Albanian to Yiddish.

Social Networks

While Google sought to transform the way people accessed information in the twenty-first century, other companies were using technology to forge links between people from all walks of life. In the 1990s the Internet had been touted as an innovative and new way to connect people—make the world a smaller place by linking people from all over the world through new websites, chat rooms, and e-mails. The new decade brought with it entrepreneurs anxious to go one step further: Give individuals the chance to have their own home on the web and stay connected to friends, acquaintances, and colleagues around the country and around the world.

One of the earliest and most popular of these so-called social networking sites was MySpace. The first version of MySpace was launched in August 2003 by techies Brad Greenspan, Chris DeWolfe, Josh Berman, and Tom Anderson, and by June 2006 MySpace was far and away the most popular social network. By the end of the decade it would have 66 million users worldwide, and its revenue from advertising would exceed $385 million. For MySpace users, the site allows them to set up their own page listing their interests and personal relationship status. They can also accrue friends or deny friendship requests, thereby exerting greater control over who sees their page content.

Another site, Facebook, began in 2004. Founded by Mark Zuckerberg, it had, by the end of the 2000s, eclipsed MySpace as the most popular social networking site with 500 million users worldwide. "What really has set Facebook apart," writes Clara Shih, "have been feeds that broadcast updates about your friends' recent activities, such as new friend connections, wall posts, photos and videos tagged of the individual, and event RSVPs."[22]

Despite the networking advantages to sites such as Facebook and MySpace, users did voice a growing concern over user privacy, fearful that identity thieves or businesses trying to sell them something could use the personal information they posted. Still, for most users, social networking sites had transformed the way they interacted with the people in their lives.

Apple's iPhone, with its touchscreen and choice of applications, or apps, enabled consumers to personalize their cell phones like never before. Pictured here is the iPhone 4, which came out in 2010 and boasts video chat, high-definition video, and sharper screen resolution.

Asian Tsunami

While technology made the lives of many easier, a colossal tragedy on December 26, 2004, provided a stark reminder of nature's power to destroy and the inability of progress to stop it. The Indian Ocean tsunami, or tidal wave, started as the third largest earthquake ever recorded. Measuring between 9.1 and 9.3 on a seismograph, its epicenter was located somewhere below the Pacific Ocean near the west coast of Sumatra, Indonesia.

Coastal areas in Indonesia, Sri Lanka, India, Malaysia, and Thailand were overwhelmed by walls of water stretching as high as 50 feet (15m). Although Indian Ocean tsunamis have been rare in recorded history, the 2004 tidal monster traveled 3,000 miles (5,000km) to the shore of Africa. The tsunami cut a path through small villages and larger cities, destroying nearly everything and leaving 225,000 people dead and millions more homeless.

Rescue efforts were hampered by poor communications and coordination of resources. For weeks, scores of corpses littered the beaches of the affected countries. As fears of post-tsunami epidemics slowly subsided, survivors slowly rebuilt their lives. Scientists also installed new early warning systems in the hope of avoiding future disasters.

Hurricane Katrina

Less than a year later, on the other side of the globe, one the world's most famous cities met an equally devastating fate. On August 29, 2005, Hurricane Katrina swept into the Gulf of Mexico and barreled toward Louisiana and Mississippi. In New Orleans, 18- to 25-foot storm surges (5.5m to 7.6m) topped the city's levee system and brought a torrent of floodwater. Before long, 80 percent of the city was under water. Thousands of people, mostly poor and African American, had no way of escaping the rising waters and found themselves trapped on pockets of dry land in an otherwise submerged city. Stranded without food or clean water, television cameras caught scores of them pleading for government assistance in the sweltering summer heat.

Two days after the storm, President Bush announced that the Federal Emergency Management Agency (FEMA) had moved 25 search and rescue teams into the New Orleans area. Yet millions of Americans watched in horror as 24-hour news coverage brought the desperation, pain, and ugliness of New Orleans into their homes: Thousands of starving and thirsty people sat stranded at the New Orleans convention center, wilting in the late summer sun; toxic chemicals poisoned the water; and gangs of criminals began roaming the streets. Three days after the storm struck, as buses finally arrived to cart victims to safety, hundreds of people were already dead. Eventually, at least 1,836 people along the Gulf died as a result of the hurricane and in the floods that followed, making it one of the deadliest storms in US history.

Criticism of the government's response to the tragedy prompted an investigation by the US Congress. The resulting 2006 report, totaling 600 pages, slammed the federal government's response to Hurricane Katrina: "If 9/11 [terrorist attacks] was a failure of imagination then Katrina was a failure of initiative," it read. "It was a failure of leadership. In this instance, blinding lack of situational awareness and disjointed decision making needlessly compounded and prolonged Katrina's horror."[23]

Climate Change Debate

In the months and years before the Asian tsunami and Hurricane Katrina, scientists had warned of disruptive global weather patterns and increased natural disasters. Industrialized countries around the world burned more fossil fuels such as coal and oil to keep their people warm and fuel their cars and trucks. Many experts argued that the "greenhouse gases" that result would prevent heat from escaping the earth's atmosphere. This "greenhouse effect," could, over time, raise the planet's temperature and put it in danger.

Scientific data from NASA and from the National Oceanic and Atmospheric Administration (NOAA) estimate that the earth's temperature has increased by 1.2 to 1.4 degrees over the last century. Consequently, significant portions of the polar ice cap—and the glaciers that supply much of the world's fresh water—are melting. The Ward Hunt Ice Shelf, a gigantic, free-floating, 3,000-year-old block of ice, once measured 155 square miles (40,145ha). In 2000 it began cracking. Two years later, it had split into two pieces.

According to Derek Mueller, a climate change expert from Trent University in Ontario, Canada, such occurrences will eventually impact the rest of the world as well. "It's a bit of a wake-up call for those people who aren't yet affected by climate change,"[24] he says. This ominous signal that the earth's climate is rapidly and, perhaps, permanently, changing, is not a universally held notion, as many skeptics refuse to tie human activity to rising temperature and melting ice floes.

In December 2009 world leaders met in Copenhagen, Denmark, with the goal of cutting fossil fuel use, but no specific deals to cut the resulting harmful gases were reached. Despite the passion and purpose among scientists around the world, governments have been slow to act. "It may seem that we'll just keep going around and around on climate change forever," writes journalist Elizabeth Kolbert. "Unfortunately, that's not the case: one day, perhaps not very long from now, the situation will spin out of our control."[25]

The technological advancement of the 2000s had transformed the lives of millions of people. Exciting new phones and handheld devices allowed consumers to stay in touch with the world as never before. The freshly mapped human genome and the growing use of stem cells opened new frontiers for scientists and medical experts. Yet no scientific breakthroughs were enough to halt nature's power to destroy. The new millennium, despite many breakthroughs, provided harsh and devastating lessons on the limits of progress.

Chapter 4

Pop Culture

Popular culture in the 2000s included a transformation of television programming, the most realistic and interactive video games ever invented, and Olympic Games that pushed the boundaries of human athleticism. The decade also produced a worldwide best seller, which followed the travails of a boy wizard and his fight against evil, and became a cultural phenomenon. In the world of professional sports, athletic achievement was often shadowed by scandals that threatened to destroy a national pastime and the new millennium's most successful sportsman.

Reality TV

By the early 2000s the popularity of made-for-cable series such as *The Sopranos* and *Project Runway* drew millions of viewers away from network television, as did the hundreds of channels viewers now had to choose from. Consequently, nervous network television executives looked to cut production costs while offering their viewers new and innovative shows that had the potential to lure TV watchers back.

Many American and European networks began experimenting with a type of programming known as reality TV. Based on popular Japanese game shows of the 1980s and 1990s, reality TV purported to film the experiences of average people in often extreme situations or in talent contests. Although such shows had been tried before, not until the introduction of two new series in the summer of 2000—*Big Brother* and *Survivor*—did reality TV become a global trend.

Big Brother, which originated in the Netherlands, placed a dozen or so contestants in a large, camera-monitored house in which they would have to live together for weeks without contact from the outside world. The rating success of the Dutch version spawned versions in Brazil, Portugal, Germany, and the United States. *Survivor*, first developed in the 1990s, dropped its contestants into a remote part of the world—typically a tropical island—and filmed them as they formed alliances, argued over chores, and voted each other off the show in a solemn tribal council ceremony. The winner was awarded $1 million. Both shows thrived on the resentment, anger, and even violence that often occurred between the contestants as the weeks wore on.

The success and longevity of *Big Brother* and *Survivor*, both of which typically led the TV ratings, encouraged producers to develop more such shows. Between 2000 and 2009 hundreds of reality shows flourished in scores of countries around the world. From *The Amazing Race* to *X-Factor* to *Supernanny*, audiences from Norway to Canada to Peru to Spain became hooked on watching people like themselves try to win millions of dollars, or fly hot air balloons, or find a mate. Still, by the end of the decade, viewers began wondering just how "real" reality TV was. J. Rupert Thompson, a director and producer of such shows, readily acknowledges putting real people into unreal situations. "What makes it so compelling is that you never know what a real person's reaction to an unreal situation will be. That's why you get such great stuff on reality TV." [26]

Music

One of the more popular reality TV shows was *American Idol*, a singing contest in which amateurs competed against one another to win a recording contract. First broadcast in the United States in 2002, the show quickly spawned similar shows around the world. The American version drew millions of viewers and became the most highly rated program on television.

Part of the show's success was owed to the talent judges, each of whom commented on singers' performances. One judge of the American version, British record executive Simon Cowell, became one of the most recognizable faces in the world, subsequently appearing in TV

Dan Brown and DaVinci

The decade's biggest literary blockbuster, Dan Brown's *The DaVinci Code*, was published in 2003 to mediocre reviews. But readers ignored the critics and gobbled up the fast-moving tale of symbologist Robert Langdon as he treks across Europe in search of a killer. Langdon's investigation begins at the Louvre, where the murder victim is posed to suggest Leonardo DaVinci's famous sketch the *Vitruvian Man*. Langdon has been called in to decipher the code. He is soon joined by police cryptographer Sophie Neveu, granddaughter of the murder victim, but he raises the suspicion of a surly French policeman named Bezu Fache. Before long Langdon and Neveu must flee from the police and are subsequently drawn into a secret world in which two clandestine groups, the Priory of Sion and Opus Dei, a devout Catholic order, are battling over the story of Jesus Christ.

Through much of the novel, the two novice detectives move from place to place, piecing the trail of clues together and eluding authorities. Mixing its suspense with an intriguing dose of religion and art, the book proved irresistible to readers around the world. *The DaVinci Code* was translated into 44 languages and sold more than 80 million copies by late 2009, making it the best-selling English language novel of the twenty-first century. The film version of the novel and its prequel, *Angels and Demons*, also proved enormously popular.

commercials and movies, including the hugely popular *Shrek* franchise. Cowell was either loved or loathed for his pointed, no-holds-barred critiques.

According to many record executives, *American Idol* reinvigorated the music industry. The numbers were difficult to argue with. Internet downloads of contestant performances sold in the millions; annual concert tours featuring each season's contestants filled stadiums across the country. Others, though, complained that *American Idol* represented everything that was wrong with music in the twenty-first century: bland songs, interchangeable performers, and misguided dreams of instant success. "The show may be fun to watch," says music journalist Bob Baker, "but it's the last place I'd recommend anyone go to learn how to succeed with a music career."[27]

Although *American Idol* may have been the biggest music story of the decade, rap and its beat-driven counterpart hip hop continued to dominate the American music charts in the 2000s. Rap also caught on in other parts of the world, influencing music makers from South Korea to London. The best-selling artist of the decade was white rapper Eminem, whose in-your-face lyrics and irresistible beats won him legions of followers for albums such as *The Slim Shady LP* and *The Eminem Show*. In all, Eminem earned 11 Grammy Awards and sold 32 million albums.

Video Games

Young people looking for other forms of entertainment during the 2000s often turned to video games. Game designers had long sought to bridge the gap between the real world and the virtual one, and now technology enabled them to get even closer to that goal. With eye-popping graphics and digital surround sound, gaming experiences such as *The Sims*, *Gran Turismo*, and *Pokemon* transformed the industry by attracting more players than ever before. In 2002 the computer game industry grew 8 percent and rang up $6.9 billion in sales. That year, video games outgrossed the movie industry for the first time in history.

No longer were video games solely geared toward children. In fact, most gamers were not children, with the average player age hovering around 29 in 2003. Much of the innovation in gaming came from Asia, specifically Japan and South Korea, where designers conjured exciting new worlds and succeeded in making game play more mainstream than ever before.

The 2000s also heralded a new age in video game interactivity. Microsoft's Xbox and Sony's PlayStation 2 systems promised and delivered some of the more realistic, high definition games ever produced. Nintendo's Wii gaming system allowed players to become more physically involved in gaming by creating Wii avatars (or versions of each player)

Eminem's in-your-face lyrics and irresistible beats won him legions of fans. The rapper, pictured performing at the 2010 Grammy Awards, earned the title of best-selling artist of the decade.

Movie Blockbuster: *Avatar*

Director James Cameron took the biggest risk of his career with his 2009 film *Avatar*. Cameron, a demanding and exacting filmmaker, had been enormously successful in movies such as *Terminator* (1984) and *Titanic* (1997), which went on to become the biggest box office hit of all time. For his new project, Cameron imagined a twenty-second-century world in which humans mine a precious mineral on a moon in a far-off galaxy. The moon is inhabited by a race of people called Na'vi, who are threatened by the mining. The humans interact with the Na'vi through the use of human-Na'vi hybrids, or avatars. Cameron had hoped to make *Avatar* in 1999, but, he later said, the technology he needed to create the innovative and exciting special effects he wanted had not yet been invented. Work on the film began in 2005, with Cameron and his team developing the Na'vi language. By 2006 the director had a complete screenplay and a budget of $237 million. *Avatar*'s release in December 2009 created a sensation, as Cameron's eye-popping use of 3-D technology and the intriguing blue color of the Na'vi attracted moviegoers around the world. After playing to months of packed movie theaters, *Avatar* became the first movie to earn $2 billion at the box office. Critics praised Cameron's vision: "He hasn't changed cinema," writes Manohla Dargis in the *New York Times,* "but with blue people and pink blooms he has confirmed its wonder."

Manohla Dargis, "A New Eden, Both Cosmic and Cinematic," *New York Times*, December 18, 2009. http://movies.nytimes.com.

called Mils with which players could serve an ace in tennis, bowl a perfect strike, or take on a phalanx of sword-wielding enemies.

Handheld games advanced as well. Particularly popular was the Nintendo DS, introduced in 2004. Primarily geared toward young people, the DS was designed as a touch screen interactive device. Fans of video games argued that playing them increased hand-eye coordination, provided players interesting moral dilemmas to sort through, and encouraged them to eat healthier food and play sports.

Detractors were more wary of the influence and popularity of video games, suggesting that hours spent in front of a screen playing often violent games dulled players' brains and encouraged antisocial behavior. Most experts agreed, though, that for children, parental guidance was essential: "Games can have many benefits," says researcher Douglas Gentile, "but parents need to help choose the games that are most likely to get maximum benefits."[28]

Tiger Woods

One of the best-selling video games of the decade took its name from golfing superstar Tiger Woods. During the 2000s Woods consistently ranked as the best golfer in the world. Young and athletic, Woods and his intense and driven style of play inspired millions of fans and pushed television ratings for the game to its highest levels ever.

In 2000 alone, Woods won 10 matches and completed a grand slam, or winning all of the major tournaments in one calendar year. "For all the greatest athletes, for all their triumphs, only a few fashion a year so magical that it exceeds our comprehension of physical (and metaphysical) superiority,"[29] writes sports journalist Frank Deford. Voted Sportsman of the Year by the editors of *Sports Illustrated* magazine, Woods was only just getting started.

Over the course of 10 years he won a total of 14 major golf championships, second only to links legend Jack Nicklaus, and 71 PGA tour events. He also became the youngest and fastest player to tally 50 tournament wins. For nearly the entire decade, Woods held the number one position in world rankings and was awarded PGA Player of the Year a record-breaking 10 times. Due to his enormous success on the field of play, Woods became a sought-after pitchman for dozens of products, from golf balls to cars to clothing, making him the richest athlete in the world. By 2009 he was earning nearly $100 million per year.

Woods was not only breaking records but racial barriers. No golfer of color had come close to reaching his level of achievement. For years, elite country clubs offered few, if any, opportunities for African Americans or other minorities. Early in his career, Woods spoke of the game's racist past and his desire to change it: "Golf has always been segregated," he said. "I've always felt golf is a game everyone should enjoy. But our goal is not just to have kids play golf, but to have strong self-esteem, then to grow up to be solid adults."[30]

Yet despite his words, Woods's place among the nation's premier athletes was tarnished in late 2009, when his marriage to model Elin Nordegren unraveled amid allegations of Woods's infidelities. The scandal that ensued at the close of the decade threatened his career as both a golfer and an advertising icon.

Baseball's Reckoning

Tiger Woods was the decade's most accomplished athlete, but in the United States, at least, baseball remained the favorite pastime in the 2000s. Yet it also had its share of setbacks.

Coming off a players' strike during the 1994 season, baseball had bounced back at the end of that decade with explosive home run displays that brought dejected fans back to the ballpark. But in March 2005, congressional hearings into illegal steroid use in baseball exposed some of the best players to withering scrutiny and harsh accusations that they had taken the drugs to enhance their performances.

Former St. Louis Cardinals slugger Mark McGwire, who had led the home run derby the decade before, was questioned about his alleged use of steroids. McGwire's evasive responses suggested that the league had not done enough to curb the taking of steroids and other performance-enhancing drugs. All of the star athletes questioned at that hearing denied using steroids, but few Americans believed them. A shadow remained over America's pastime, as baseball commissioner

Bud Selig made a commitment to crack down on players who tested positive for steroid use.

Selig's promise notwithstanding, the congressional investigations continued. In 2008 seven-time Cy Young–winning pitcher Roger Clemens also denied using steroids. Clemens's testimony provided a stark contrast

Golf superstar Tiger Woods was consistently ranked as the world's best golfer during the 2000s. His intense style of play inspired millions of fans until personal scandal threatened both his career and his appeal to advertisers.

to that of his personal former trainer, Brian McNamee, who told the House committee that he had personally injected Clemens with steroids and human growth hormone (HGH). Many committee members, like the public, did not want to believe that an athlete of Clemens's caliber could have taken steroids, but many found his countless denials unconvincing. "It's hard to believe you, sir," said Representative Elijah Cummings. "I hate to say that. You're one of my heroes. But it's hard to believe."[31] Cummings's statement was echoed by millions of baseball fans, many of whom wondered how the ongoing scandal would affect the game's future.

Beijing Olympics

Steroids in baseball were a concern primarily in the United States, but performance-enhancing drugs in the Olympics Games were the world's problem. The International Olympic Committee had set the standard for drug testing and disqualified many athletes for testing positive for steroids in the past.

Despite this shadow over the summer and winter games, the best athletes from around the globe continued to compete at the highest levels of athletic achievement during the 2000s. Perhaps the most exciting Olympic games of the new millennium were held in Beijing, China, in the summer of 2008. The location itself promised to turn China, at least temporarily, into a major sports power. The country had spent millions of dollars building new sporting facilities and preparing to host more than 11,000 athletes from 203 nations.

The Beijing Olympics attracted the largest television audience in the games' history. Competitors broke 43 world records and 132 Olympic records, with China pulling in 100 medals, 51 of them gold. In total medals won, China was bested only by the United States, which earned 110. The undisputed superstar of the Beijing games was American swimmer Michael Phelps, who won eight gold medals and broke the seven gold medals record of American Mark Spitz at the 1972 Munich games. The other athlete to dominate the games was Jamaican sprinter Usain Bolt, who broke world records and won gold medals in the 100-meter and 200-meter races, and, with his teammates, the 4x100-meter relay. No other runner had ever accomplished such a feat.

The Harry Potter Phenomenon

The literary feat of the decade was that of J.K. Rowling and her fictional invention Harry Potter. Conceived on a train trip through England and written partly in an Edinburgh coffee shop while her baby daughter slept, Rowling's series of novels about a boy wizard and his friends was rejected by a dozen British publishing houses before given a chance by Bloomsbury.

The publisher suggested the young author use her initials rather than her given name of Joanne because it feared that boys might not want to read a book written by a woman. In 1997 the first Potter novel *The Sorcerer's Stone (Philosopher's Stone* in Great Britain) had an initial press run of only 1,000 copies. A year later the American rights were sold for $105,000. The book's popularity quickly exploded and propelled the 32-year-old author into a life of worldwide fame and enormous wealth.

During the 2000s the six books that followed sold 400 million copies worldwide; the movie versions took in over $1 billion at the box office. This phenomenal success earned Rowling nearly $800 million, making her the twelfth richest woman in Great Britain. After finishing the final book in the series, *Harry Potter and the Deathly Hallows* in 2007, Rowling turned much of her attention to supporting charitable causes that fight poverty and multiple sclerosis, an inflammatory disease.

Yet Rowling's most lasting contribution may well have been her story's power to get young people reading. "Harry Potter has helped to overcome this resistance to reading for many children," write educators Vicki L. Cohen and John E. Cowen, "and encouraged parents to sit and read the books aloud to those not yet capable of reading them independently."[32]

The success of the Harry Potter series marked a high point in the decade's pop culture pantheon. But the talented boy wizard could not cast a spell on the decade's political and economic fortunes. These were fraught with peril and uncertainty and threatened to erase any progress made in the young century.

Chapter 5

Economic and Political Upheaval

The decade of the 2000s began in economic scandal. It ended in economic disaster for many nations and millions of people around the world. Banking systems in Great Britain, France, Germany, Japan, and the United States neared collapse in 2008 and 2009. Worldwide calamity was avoided only by governments pumping trillions of dollars into their financial systems. Nevertheless, the damage had been done and brought financial ruin to average people in all corners of the globe, many of whom saw their savings collapse, their credit dry up, and their homes foreclosed.

Politically, the United States witnessed the historic election of the nation's first African American president. Barack Obama's rise to power gave people throughout the world hope that they could bring about dramatic political change in their lifetimes. But free and fair elections continued to be the exception in many countries.

The Fall of Enron

The first genuine financial scandal of the decade was revealed in October 2001. The collapse of the Enron Corporation, an American energy company, rattled the US economy and devastated employee retirement savings. Founded in 1985 by Kenneth Lay, the company exploited accounting and tax loopholes to hide financial losses from its board of directors and its workers. "The Enron scandal grew out of a steady accumulation of habits and values and actions that began years before and finally spiraled out of control,"[33] write journalists Bethany McLean and Peter Elkind.

McLean's reporting for *Fortune* magazine suggested in March 2001 that Enron's value could be overpriced, since she discovered that its earnings did not match its high stock value. She also reported on the company's large debt and unusual accounting practices. Lay and Enron president Jeffrey Skilling defended their corporation, but investors lost faith in the company, and its stock price began to fall. In late November

Barack Obama, the nation's first African American president, speaks at a White House news conference. Obama took office in 2009, marking a historic moment in US history.

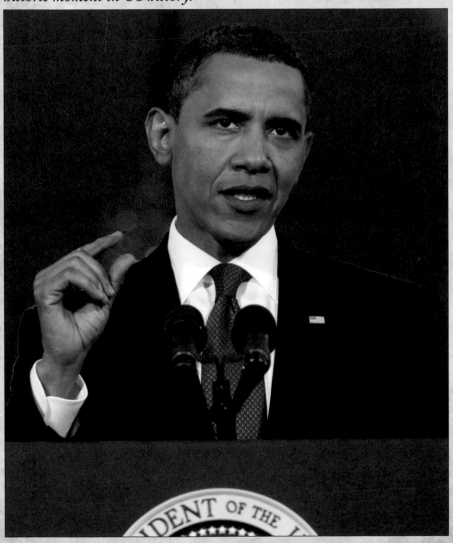

the company filed for bankruptcy. Its stock was now trading for less than $1; its losses were estimated at $23 billion.

Enron executives were charged with various counts of money laundering, fraud, and insider stock trading. Skilling and Lay went on trial in 2006. Skilling was convicted of 19 of the 28 counts against him and was sentenced to 24 years in prison. Lay, who pleaded not guilty, was convicted on 6 counts of securities and wire fraud and faced a sentence of 45 years behind bars. He died suddenly on July 5, 2006, before the final sentence was announced. Arthur Andersen, the accounting firm that had helped Enron hide its losses and cheat its investors, was found guilty of obstructing justice. It subsequently closed its doors; 85,000 employees lost their jobs.

The downfall of Enron, which illustrated corporate greed at its worst, appeared at first to be an isolated incident. But in fewer than 10 years, a global recession, high unemployment, and a depressed housing market would make Enron look like a warm-up to these conditions.

Recession 2008

In February 2007 the housing market in the United States—which had boomed for much of the decade—turned sour. In April, mortgage lender New Century Financial filed for bankruptcy, signaling that all was not well. Soon other lenders, including Countrywide, the nation's largest, were having serious financial trouble.

As spring turned to summer, credit markets declined steeply as companies that offered credit to consumers ran low on funds. The European Central Bank tried to stop the credit crunch by injecting billions of Euros into the system, but virtually nothing could stop the dramatic decline. Economists were wary; not all were convinced that the downturn in the economy would last. "The recession is likely to last two to three quarters and should be relatively mild by historical standards, with a cumulative decline in real GDP of only about a half percent,"[34] Goldman Sachs economists Jan Hatzius and Ed McKelvey said in January 2008. Neither could have predicted that the recession would be deeper and last far longer.

Financial institutions around the world were not alone in feeling the pain of the global recession that began in 2008. Ordinary people lost their jobs and their homes in record numbers. American home foreclosures surpassed 3 million in 2008 and the ruinous slide continued for the rest of the decade.

While politicians in Washington, DC, argued over how best to save a cratered economy, millions of Americans were consumed with how to keep a roof over their heads. Sandra Hines, a lifetime resident of Detroit, Michigan, in 2008 lost the family home she shared with her sister because they could no longer afford its adjustable rate mortgage. After months of desperately trying to save their residence from foreclosure, the sisters were evicted a week before Christmas. Like the Hines sisters, Pat Weber worried about keeping her home. The resident of Fennville, Michigan, lost her job as a construction administrator and could not find another—even after applying for more than 100 positions. At 58, and with few employment prospects, Weber put her two-bedroom house on the market. She feared she would not be able to make the mortgage payments for much longer. Unfortunately, she found no buyers. "This is so debilitating, so humiliating," she said. "I feel kicked to the curb. It's been one defeat after another, seems like forever. I feel reduced to nothing."

Quoted in Susan Saulny and Monica Davey, "New Economic Fears Arise in Michigan," *New York Times*, November 22, 2008. www.nytimes.com.

In March 2008 the US government promised to rescue Morgan Chase with a $30 billion loan at the low interest rate of 3.25 percent. This so-called "bailout" by the federal government was only the beginning. In September, mortgage lenders Fannie Mae and Freddie Mac also turned to the US government in desperation. The George W. Bush administration had little choice but to help the giant companies, which owned or guaranteed $5.3 trillion worth of mortgages.

For a time, the government took ownership of the struggling Fannie and Freddie, making it the largest bailout in American history. Rejecting calls by some in his own political party to let the lenders go out of business, Bush said, "Putting these companies on sound financial footing, and reforming their business practices, is critical to the health of our financial system."[35]

Bad and Getting Worse

The autumn crisis only deepened and continued into the winter and spring of 2009. Already deeply in debt and with two wars costing nearly $900 billion, the Bush administration was trying anything to keep the financial markets from collapsing into a new Great Depression, and it had hard choices to make. In early October the US House of Representatives acted, approving a $700 billion bailout to the country's financial sector. The goal was to stabilize the sinking ship of state; legislators and the president hoped that it would work. Georgia Democrat John Lewis spoke for many in the chamber when he said, "I have decided that the cost of doing nothing is greater than the cost of doing something."[36]

The government action was not popular among all Americans. Indeed, many were angered by reports of high executive compensation in the banking industry. This only added to the general feeling of distrust that people had for both the federal government and financial institutions. Much of the growing animosity stemmed from the rising unemployment rate, which reached 10 percent in 2008. Without jobs, many people found it nearly impossible to pay their mortgages. Between 2008 and 2009 at least 1.2 million Americans lost their homes to foreclosure; 2.6 million fell into poverty.

One of them, 49-year-old business consultant Richard Brown was out of work for more than a year and soon found he could not pay his mortgage. Forced to relocate, he found a room in a local boardinghouse. But the situation was less than ideal. "I pay $600 for a third-floor room that gets hot in the summer," he said. "It's a blow. I don't belong here.

I'm an educated person. I've held executive positions. And here I am in a boarding house."[37]

Brown's story was repeated countless times, not only in the United States but around the world. Europe's once thriving economy quickly turned sour in the wake of the US recession. Germany, Italy, Ireland, and Denmark fared the worst, as banks collapsed and hundreds of thousands of workers found themselves out of work. In Asia, too, slow economic growth translated into fewer people spending money. In Japan, where corporate profits dropped sharply, government officials worried about what the global recession would mean for their country.

China's booming economy was relatively unscathed by the global economic crisis that took root in 2008 but the world's most populous nation faces other challenges. One is pollution. Among China's polluted waterways is the Yangtze River (pictured), which supplies drinking water to hundreds of cities.

Bernard L. Madoff was one of the first people to imagine a trading world in which investors could purchase stocks electronically and on the Internet. Yet in 2005 investigator Harry Markopolos sent a report to the US Securities and Exchange Commission (SEC) strongly suggesting that Madoff was running the world's largest Ponzi scheme. Madoff, according to Markopolos, took clients' money and rather than investing it and earning a profit, returned it to them or to other clients while taking a large portion of the money for himself. Despite accusations that Madoff was doing exactly this, the SEC took no action. In late 2008, growing economic instability destroyed Madoff's business and his clients' savings along with it. Madoff confessed his dishonesty to his sons, Mark and Andrew. Soon after, FBI agents arrested Madoff and charged him with securities fraud.

In all, the former titan of Wall Street had stolen nearly $65 billion. The victims of his greed included Holocaust survivors, movie stars, and average working people who had trusted Madoff with their money and lost it all. On March 12, 2009, Madoff entered a New York City courtroom and pleaded guilty to 11 federal charges, including wire fraud, mail fraud, and money laundering. Madoff also spoke of his crime and apologized to the people whose lives he had ruined, but Madoff's remorse had little influence on the jury that convicted him or the judge who sentenced him to 150 years behind bars.

The Rise of China

Another Asian nation, China, was one of the few countries left relatively unscathed by the global economic morass. Over the course of the decade the Chinese government built up its infrastructure and workforce. From high-speed rail lines to soaring high-rises, China put millions of people to work and became a financial powerhouse in the world.

As Americans were reeling from an economy spiraling out of control, they may not have noticed this new economic power rising in the East. China, once a sleeping fiscal giant, had woken up. With over 1 billion people—compared to 300 million Americans—China's potential frightened many in the West. In particular, its investments in the United States, along with its monetary policy and booming productivity, threatened the world's last superpower.

During the 2000s China's economy grew at least 10 percent per year, a staggering number, and in the nearly 30 years before that, 400 million Chinese were lifted out of poverty. Such growth surprised many economists, in part because China is an authoritarian state, run by the Communist Party. Still, says journalist James Kynge, China "has succeeded in fostering a capitalist economy so vibrant that in many ways it outcompetes America."[38]

The rise of modern cities transformed China in various ways. Young people from all over the country flocked to urban areas to attend college or find better, more lucrative jobs. By doing so, a new generation bridged many centuries of developmental time and helped propel China's economy into a seemingly unstoppable force.

Pollution and Productivity

One effect of China's growing power and status was a rise in pollution of all sorts. The country's longest river, the Yangtze, was called "cancerous" by scientists. The drinking water of nearly 200 cities along its banks was contaminated with the runoff from shipbuilding, papermaking, and chemical waste. By the end of the decade, reports suggested that 70 percent of the Yangtze's water was dangerous to consume. Air pollution is so toxic in some Chinese cities that as many as 380,000 people die from it each year.

Despite these setbacks, at decade's end China remained a force, inspired in large part by the American dream. Chinese billionaire Jack Ma has cultivated this idea of success and progress, as founder of Alibaba,

China's largest e-commerce website. The key to China's future, and perhaps that of the United States, is decisiveness, he says: "When I go there [to America], they are building up a road, and they discuss for two or three years without deciding. But China? Well, let's make it happen. . . . I look at many of the nations moving so slowly. China, at least we move fast. Make a decision quick, and we have a culture of doing that."[39]

Election of Obama

Worldwide financial catastrophe loomed throughout 2008, but so did a presidential election in the United States. Voters would soon be forced to decide whether to continue the financial policies of the previous eight years or cast a vote for change. As Bush's term in office slowly came to an end, polls suggested that the American public was vastly unhappy with its president. A Gallup poll in the fall of 2008 said that only 25 percent of Americans approved of how the president handled his job; 75 percent disapproved.

The candidates vying for Bush's job could hardly have been more different. Long-time Arizona senator and Vietnam War veteran John McCain had earned the nickname "the Maverick" for his willingness to cross political party lines. Illinois senator Obama, an African American from Chicago, built his presidential campaign on the themes of hope and change. Obama's eloquent speeches, knowledge of the issues, and placid exterior had won him many admirers. Many voters, who knew all too well their nation's history of racial inequality, were also inspired by the idea of electing the nation's first black president.

On Election Day, calls for change trumped a return to former policies. Obama collected 52.9 percent of the popular vote to McCain's 45.7 percent. He had bested his opponent in many traditionally Republican states such as Virginia and North Carolina. As he greeted his supporters in Chicago's Grant Park after his victory, the first African American president-elect in US history captured the thoughts of many: "If there is anyone out there who still doubts that America is a place where all things are possible, who still wonders if the dream of our founders is alive in our time, who still questions the power of our democracy, tonight is your answer."[40]

Mired in an economic crisis, a majority of Americans had voted for change, for a new way forward. But Obama's promises of financial reform, health care for all, and lower unemployment had yet to be realized. Only the coming years would tell whether they would be.

Protests in Iran

The historic election of Obama had been celebrated throughout the world, but in June 2009 the presidential election in Iran ended in protests. The Islamic republic's incumbent president Mahmoud Ahmadinejad had caused alarm in the past with belligerent statements toward Iran's neighbor Israel. The Iranian government also had made headlines across the globe by seeking nuclear materials for, they claimed, peaceful energy purposes. But many in the community of nations believed the country also wanted to build nuclear weapons.

Thousands of people protest the outcome of Iran's 2009 presidential election, which was said to be tainted by fraudulent results. To curb spreading protests, the government temporarily closed universities and blocked websites used by organizers of the demonstrations.

The 2009 election, according to experts, was an important one that could change the political equation and prove helpful in convincing Iran to reveal its true nuclear ambitions. Ahmadinejad's opponent, Mir Hossein Moussavi, was considered a more moderate candidate. When the election results were tabulated, Ahmadinejad had 63 percent of the vote to Moussavi's 34 percent. Moussavi's supporters cried foul, claiming that their votes had been left uncounted or thrown out.

Thousands took to the streets, setting trash cans on fire and shouting for justice. Such antigovernment demonstrations had rarely been seen in the capital city of Tehran. Cell phone cameras captured the protests, the videos of which were then posted to YouTube, Facebook, and Twitter. In the weeks and months that followed, this so-called "Green Revolution" continued as protests flared. The Iranian government claimed that 36 people died during the violence. Moussavi supporters put the figure at 72. To curb the protests, Iran temporarily closed universities in Tehran and blocked websites used by protest organizers.

The elections in the United States and in Iran provided stark political contrasts. While Obama's victory reflected an orderly and peaceful transition of power, the Green Revolution in Iran provided a window into a political process in which democracy and the rule of law remained at odds.

Chapter 6 🌐

What Is the Legacy of the 2000s?

"The past is another country," novelist L.P. Hartley once wrote. "They do things differently there."[41] Still, those who make an effort to understand the past may find a path forward to the future. The decade of the 2000s brought terrorism and war. The conflicts in Iraq and Afghanistan raged on, and religious extremism remained a threat to people around the world. Scientists succeeded in mapping the human genome, while innovators developed advances in technology that made communication easier and faster. Still, people in distress struggled to have their voices heard after disasters in New Orleans, Indonesia, and Thailand. Artists created new works that entertained and enthralled; China and Brazil flexed their economic muscles while other nations faltered; and the world's oldest democracy elected an African American to the presidency 146 years after freeing its last black slave. In the end, the progress—even the setbacks—of the first 10 years of the new millennium laid the foundation for the changes and challenges of the decades to follow.

Continued Growth

Even during the worldwide recession in which millions of jobs and homes were lost, a handful of nations remained economically stable and promised to gain strength in the second decade of the twenty-first century. In East Asia and Latin America, especially, economies grew and prospered.

In China, part of this new financial power could be tied to China's devaluing its currency, the yuan. This made it cheaper for China to

US soldiers take cover in Iraq. The violence and conflict that raged throughout the first decade of the 2000s in Iraq and Afghanistan continued into the next decade.

produce, export, and sell goods that people around the world wanted to buy. The nation's yearly 10 percent growth showed few signs of slowing, but China was not the only Asian economy on the move. India's consumer culture exploded by the decade's end, and India itself stood second only to the United States in level of consumption of goods and services. The quality of products produced in India has also improved in recent decades. "The old assumption that 'made in India' means second-rate is disappearing," says journalist Fareed Zakaria. "Indian companies are buying stakes in Western companies because they think they can do a better job of managing them."[42] According to Zakaria, in 2006 and 2007 Indian investment in Great Britain, its former colonizer, was larger than British investment in India.

On the other side of the world, Latin America became an economic force to be reckoned with. In the continent's largest country, Brazil, the economy grew 7.5 percent in 2010. It also built a healthy financial surplus and remained politically stable. This, according to analyst Ian Bremmer, suggests continued economic success. The country's "stable democratic governance have created a solid foundation for steady and predictable growth over the next several years,"[43] he says. Brazil's Latin American neighbors Argentina, Peru, and Paraguay also posted growth and forged closer ties with Asian markets.

Despite challenges to their economic supremacy, American and European experts remained hopeful that their nations would regain strength after two years of crippling recession. "When they look back on this cascade of catastrophes, Americans in the future will assume our lives were miserable, practically unlivable," says historian Gil Troy. "Yet, for most of us, life has continued. We have maintained our routines, while watching these disasters unfold on the news. In fact, these have been relatively good years. America remains the world's playground, the most prolific, most excessive platform for shopping and fun in human history."[44]

Ongoing War: Iraq and Afghanistan

As the new Obama administration settled into the White House, stark decisions had to be made about ongoing wars in Afghanistan and Iraq. Violence in Iraq had dropped dramatically by late 2007 as Sunni Muslims lowered their weapons and joined what soon became known as the Sunni Awakening. "At the beginning, people saw it as an occupation which had to be resisted," explains militia leader Abul Abed, "But then, they saw that the Americans were working in the interest of the people. They saw al Qaeda doing terrible things."[45]

With violence in Iraq declining, Obama worked to bring the conflict to an end. In February 2009 he declared that combat operations would cease in 18 months. In August 2010 the president announced a reduction of troops in Iraq from 144,000 to below 50,000. Whether the violence would return once all US soldiers departed remained to be seen. Some experts worried that Iraq's central government was too fragile to keep order; others believed the United States could do little more for the fledgling democracy.

Afghanistan, meanwhile, remained a violent and lawless country. According to the new president, Iraq had been the wrong war; Afghanistan, the country where Bin Laden had planned the 9/11 attacks, was the necessary war. In the first year of his presidency, Obama ordered a 17,000-troop increase to help calm the troubled country and to keep al Qaeda from reorganizing itself there. "This increase is necessary to stabilize a deteriorating situation in Afghanistan, which has not received the strategic attention, direction and resources it urgently requires,"[46] Obama said in February 2009. The president's decision to temporarily raise troop levels proved controversial with the American people, many of whom cared less about a distant war than they did about the jobs and economic security many of them had lost in the recession.

Despite the administration's emphasis on Afghanistan, the most pressing foreign policy issue was the impact of its neighbor Pakistan. Although the United States considered the nuclear-armed nation an ally in the fight against al Qaeda, the country's government was less than stable, and strong evidence suggested that the country was harboring Osama bin Laden and fellow terror masterminds in its region bordering Afghanistan. On May 2, 2011, the Obama administration acted on that evidence. That night, US Navy SEALS, a highly-trained group of commandos, raided a residential compound in Abbottabad, Pakistan, and shot and killed Osama bin Laden. Hours later, his body was buried at sea. Days later, al Qaeda vowed revenge.

Fight for Gay Rights

Domestically, the economy occupied the minds of most Americans. But other issues, including the rights of gay Americans, also proved important. A grassroots movement to ensure homosexuals the same civil rights as heterosexuals began growing in the 1960s. Four decades later, this determined activism would pave the way for broader acceptance of homosexuals in both the American military and in society at large.

Piracy in Somalia

Ⓞne dangerous legacy of the 2000s is the world's virtual ignorance (and some might say neglect) of Somalia, a war-torn African nation that slipped into absolute lawlessness during the decade. A costly—and deadly—result of ignoring events in Somalia has been the rise of piracy. "Fundamentally, the piracy problem off the Somali coast arises out of the fundamental problem of statelessness on shore," says J. Peter Pham, director of the Nelson Institute for International and Public Affairs at James Madison University. "Without effective governing on shore you're going to have opportunities for criminals to engage in their enterprises with impunity." Out-of-work and desperate Somali fishermen whose resources are often plundered by neighboring nations ride the waves in speedboats, hop aboard freighters that appear promising, and brandish machine guns and machetes at terrified sailors.

By mid-decade, Somali pirates had hijacked hundreds of ships, demanding ransoms of up to $20 million. In February 2011, pirates from Somalia murdered four Americans who were sailing their yachts in the Indian Ocean. Despite international calls for UN intervention, experts believe that the only solution to the problem of Somali piracy is a stable government that provides for its poverty-stricken people. But Somalia's problems echo that of many other African nations, whose people are desperate and disenfranchised. These ongoing problems also make such countries vulnerable to terrorist groups such as al Qaeda, who hide there and use them to plot their next attacks.

Quoted in "Somali Piracy—Causes and Consequences," *Voice of America*, April 10, 2009. www. voanews.com.

In 2003 the Massachusetts Supreme Judicial Court ruled that the state must allow homosexual couples to marry. This controversial decision set off shockwaves among conservative groups across the country and celebrations among supporters of gay rights.

The issue subsequently took the national stage. Gay marriage opponents in Arizona, California, and Florida made their voices heard in November 2008 by voting to amend their state constitutions to ban gay marriage. Christian groups were particularly adamant and often pointed to biblical teachings as reasons why gay marriage is against the laws of God and man.

Yet supporters of gay marriage appeared to be growing in size by the end of the 2000s. By 2008, over 50 percent of people in at least three states supported gay marriage, often arguing that heterosexual couples have many more rights than their gay counterparts, including tax breaks, access to a partner's health insurance, the right to visit a sick partner in the hospital, death benefits, and joint ownership of property.

This growing social acceptance and call for increased gay rights also affected the American military's "Don't Ask, Don't Tell" policy. Developed and voted into law in the 1990s during the Clinton years, this policy, in effect, demanded that gay soldiers hide their homosexuality or be forced out of military service.

With the election of Obama, supporters of the law's repeal had reason to hope that the new president would work on their behalf. During the 2008 campaign, Obama came down strongly in favor of an end to the "Don't Ask, Don't Tell" policy. "We're spending large sums of money to kick highly qualified gays or lesbians out of our military," he said, "some of whom possess specialties like Arab-language capabilities that we desperately need. That doesn't make us more safe."[47]

Many, though, were initially disappointed by the Obama administration's failure to make the repeal of "Don't Ask, Don't Tell" a cornerstone of its public policy. Then in the fall of 2010, irreversible cracks in the law resulted from a series of court decisions and a Pentagon study that suggested that ending the policy would have little impact on national security. In December 2010 both chambers of the US Congress passed a repeal of "Don't Ask, Don't Tell." The various branches of the

American military soon after committed themselves to ending the policy once and for all. How the change might affect the nation's ongoing military commitments remained unclear as the new decade began.

Obama and the Tea Party

Obama's history-making election in 2008 gave way to other real challenges facing the United States. With two wars and a sputtering economy, the promise of immediate change quickly dwindled. In 2008 and 2009 American unemployment stood near 10 percent, and a once booming housing market had gone bust, leaving millions of Americans owing more money on their mortgages than their homes were worth.

After more than a year in office, Obama's luster had begun to fade with many voters. The ranks of Obama detractors steadily increased. Thousands joined what came to be known as the Tea Party movement, which originally took its name from the acronym Taxed Enough Already

The US policy of "Don't Ask, Don't Tell" required gays in the military to hide their homosexuality or be forced out of military service. Growing social acceptance of gay rights led Congress to repeal the policy in December 2010. Protestors urge repeal of the policy in a demonstration a few months earlier.

Black Political Candidates

Barack Obama's election to the American presidency not only inspired his supporters, it also encouraged other African Americans to run for high office. Yet in many cases, those seeking office were from the opposite end of the political spectrum. In November 2010 more than 30 black Republicans ran for seats in the US Congress. Two of them, Allen West and Tim Scott, won. Their victories in Florida and South Carolina, respectively, marked a small but important shift in the political landscape.

Traditionally, an overwhelming majority of African Americans were Democrats and voted accordingly. But this new breed of political powerhouses made it clear that on fiscal and social issues they strongly disagreed with the president and the direction in which he was taking the country. Instead, organizations like the National Black Republican Association looked to figures such as former secretary of state Condoleezza Rice and Supreme Court justice Clarence Thomas for inspiration. Still, political insider Dean Nelson says that despite policy differences, it was Obama's historic election that gave African American conservatives reason to believe in themselves: "I think with his success, it has given a level of hope and expectation for African-American candidates, whether they're Republican or Democrat that you know hey, this is something that can be done."

Quoted in Alex Pappas, "Obama Inspires Black Politicians to Seek Office—as Republican Candidates," *Daily Caller*, March 25, 2010. http://dailycaller.com.

and was inspired by the antitaxation Boston tea party of 1773. Tea partiers demanded that Washington curb its spending and keep taxes low. "The Tea Party was an authentic popular movement," writes journalist Kate Zernike, "brought on by anger over the economy and distrust of government—at all levels, and in both parties."[48]

Adherents, most of whom identified with the Republican party, also claimed a deep-seated belief in what they interpreted as the original principles of the American constitution. Often stoked into a furor by conservative commentators like Rush Limbaugh and Glenn Beck, the tea partiers held rallies and worked to elect like-minded politicians. They did so in November 2010 when midterm elections swept dozens of Tea Party–supported candidates into office, shifting the majority in the House of Representatives in favor of Republicans and making the Democratic majority in the Senate razor thin.

The political atmosphere in Washington, DC, thus remained more divisive than ever. While Republican leaders called Obama's policies bad for the country, Democrats accused Republicans of obstructing the president's agenda. Although Obama had campaigned on a promise of changing Washington, DC, many argued that it was changing him.

Looking Forward

The 2000s proved to be a challenging decade for much of the world. Violence in the African nation of Sudan remained ever present; authoritarian rule persisted in Burma, now known as Myanmar, as it did across the Middle East in Egypt, Jordan, and Saudi Arabia. As the next decade of the twenty-first century dawned, economic and social unrest appeared unlikely to disappear in the near future.

Still, the 2000s and its lessons had much to teach about the next phase of the still-young century. In 2009 journalist Joel Achenbach acknowledged the decade's difficult journey but also sounded a hopeful note: "As history marches on, this decade will be known for its stumbles and reversals," he writes. "The scolds and doubters reminded us that hope is not a plan. But neither is despair a winning strategy. The smart move is to look back at the 2000s glancingly, and then turn, with optimism, to the decade ahead."[49]

Source Notes

Introduction: The Defining Characteristics of the 2000s

1. Andy Serwer, "The '00s: Goodbye (at Last) to the Decade from Hell," *Time*, November 24, 2009. www.time.com.
2. Joel Achenbach, "Joel Achenbach on the 2000s: The Decade We Didn't See Coming," *Washington Post*, December 27, 2009. www.washingtonpost.com.

Chapter One: What Events Led into the 2000s?

3. William Shakespeare, *The Tempest*. New York: Penguin, 1998, p. 121.
4. Quoted in PBS, *The Gulf War*, transcript, 1996. www.pbs.org.
5. Quoted in PBS, *The Gulf War*.
6. Quoted in Lawrence Wright, *The Looming Tower: Al-Qaeda and the Road to 9/11*. New York: Alfred K. Knopf, 2006, p. 4.
7. Quoted in Wright, *The Looming Tower*, p. 6.
8. Quoted in Nicole Nichols, "Domestic Terrorism 101: Timothy James McVeigh," *Eye on Hate*, 2003. www.eyeonhate.com.

Chapter Two: Politics, War, and Terrorism

9. Quoted in Howard Gillman, *The Votes That Counted: How the Court Decided the 2000 Presidential Election*. Chicago: University of Chicago Press, 2003, p. 1.
10. Quoted in Stephen Gale, Michael Radu, and Harvey Sicherman, *The War on Terrorism: 21st Century Perspectives*. New York: Transaction, 2009, p. 66.
11. Quoted in CNN, "Transcript of President Bush's Address," September 21, 2001. http://articles.cnn.com.
12. Ahmed Rashid, *Taliban: Militant Islam, Oil, and Fundamentalism in Central Asia*. New Haven, CT: Yale University Press, 2010, p. 237.

13. Quoted in Demetrios Caraley, *American Hegemony: Preventive War, Iraq, and Imposing Democracy*. New York: Academy of Political Science, 2004, p. 39.

14. Quoted in *BBC News*, "London Bomber: Text in Full," September 1, 2005. http://news.bbc.co.uk.

15. Quoted in *BBC News*, "Mumbai Rocked by Deadly Attacks," November 27, 2008. http://news.bbc.co.uk.

16. Quoted in Martin Fackler, "South Koreans Express Fatigue with a Recalcitrant North," *New York Times*, May 27, 2009. www.nytimes.com.

Chapter Three: Science, Technology, and the Power of Nature

17. Alison Bashford and Philippa Levine, *The Oxford Handbook of the History of Eugenics*. New York: Oxford University Press, 2010, p. 93.

18. Hank Bordowitz, *Dirty Little Secrets of the Record Business: Why So Much Music You Hear Sucks*. Chicago: Chicago Review, 2007, p. 56.

19. Brent Schendler, "Perspective: The App-Phone Revolution Is Well Underway. So Where's Microsoft?," *BNET*, December 9, 2009. www.bnet.com.

20. Megan McArdle, "Old Media Blues," *Atlantic*, July 1, 2009. www.theatlantic.com.

21. Rick Kash and David Calhoun, *How Companies Win: Profiting from Demand-Driven Business Models No Matter What Business You're In*. New York: HarperBusiness, 2010.

22. Clara Shih, *The Facebook Era: Tapping Online Social Networks to Build Better Products, Reach New Audiences, and Sell More Stuff*. Indianapolis: Prentice-Hall, 2009, p. 36.

23. Quoted in Dan Glaister, "Republicans Brand Katrina Response a National Failure," *The Guardian*, February 13, 2006. www.guardian.co.uk

24. Quoted in David Ljunggren, "Giant Chunks Break Off Canadian Ice Shelf," *Reuters*, July 29, 2008. www.reuters.com.

25. Elizabeth Kolbert, "Uncomfortable Climate," *New Yorker*, November 22, 2010. www.newyorker.com.

Chapter Four: Pop Culture

26. Quoted in Michael Ventre, "Just How Real Are Reality TV Shows?" *Today*, April 14, 2009. http://today.msnbc.msn.com.

27. Bob Baker, "What's Wrong with *American Idol?*," *Vocalist*, 2008. www.vocalist.org.uk.

28. Quoted in Tech Shout, "Video Games Encourage Positive Behavior: Study," April 7, 2009. www.techshout.com.

29. Frank Deford, "Sportsman of the Year," *Sports Illustrated*, December 18, 2000. http://sportsillustrated.cnn.com.

30. Quoted in Blaine T. Browne and Robert C. Cottrell, *American Lives*. Armonk, NY: M.E. Sharpe, 2008, p. 311.

31. Quoted in Associated Press, "Clemens, McNamee Get Grilled by Congress," *NBC Sports*, February 14, 2008. http://nbcsports.msnbc.com.

32. Vicki L. Cohen and John E. Cowen, *Literacy for Children in an Information Age: Teaching, Writing, and Thinking*. Detroit: Cengage, 2010, p. 403.

Chapter Five: Economic and Political Upheaval

33. Bethany McLean and Peter Elkind, *The Smartest Guys in the Room: The Amazing Rise and Scandalous Fall of Enron*. New York: Portfolio, 2003, p. 132.

34. Quoted in *CBS News Business*, "Goldman Sachs: Brace for Recession in 2008," January 9, 2008. www.cbsnews.com.

35. Quoted in *BBC News*, "US Takes Over Key Mortgage Firms," September 7, 2008. http://news.bbc.co.uk.

36. Quoted in *BBC News*, "House Backs $700bn [Billion] Bail-Out Plan," October 3, 2008. http://news.bbc.co.uk.

37. Quoted in John W. Schoen, "Study: 1.2 Million Households Lost to Recession," MSNBC, April 8, 2008. www.msnbc.msn.com.

38. James Kynge, *China Shakes the World*. Boston: Houghton Mifflin, 2006, p. xv.

39. Quoted in Bradley Blackburn, "Chinese Billionaire Jack Ma on the Power of American Ideas," *ABC World News*, November 15, 2010.

40. Quoted in CNN, "Transcript: 'This Is Your Victory,' Says Obama," November 4, 2008. http://articles.cnn.com.

Chapter Six: What Is the Legacy of the 2000s?

41. Quoted in Michael Wood, *The Road to Delphi: The Life and Afterlife of Oracles*. New York: Macmillan, 2004, p. 7.

42. Fareed Zakaria, *The Post-American World*. New York: Norton, 2008, p. 137.

43. Ian Bremmer, "Brazil's Economic Growth Shouldn't Be Overlooked," *Huffington Post*, October 17, 2007. www.huffingtonpost.com.

44. Quoted in Achenbach, "Joel Achenbach on the 2000s."

45. Quoted in John Hendren, "'Sunni Awakening': Insurgents Are Now Allies," *ABC News*, December 23, 2007. http://abcnews.go.com.

46. Quoted in Barbara Starr, "Obama Approves Afghanistan Troop Increase," CNN, February 17, 2009.

47. Quoted in Associated Press, "Obama: Repeal of 'Don't Ask, Don't Tell' Possible," MSNBC, April 10, 2008. www.msnbc.msn.com.

48. Kate Zernike, *Boiling Mad: Inside Tea Party America*. New York: Times Books, 2010, p. 3.

49. Achenbach, "Joel Achenbach on the 2000s."

Important People of the 2000s

Osama bin Laden: A Saudi millionaire who founded al Qaeda, an Islamic terrorist organization. He helped organize and plot dozens of attacks on civilians and military personnel around the world, including the bombing of the USS *Cole* in 2000 and the 9/11 attacks in 2001. He was killed by US forces in May 2011.

George W. Bush: The forty-third president of the United States, from 2001 to 2009. Bush's time in office was marked by the US invasion of Iraq; large tax cuts and high deficits; the passing of No Child Left Behind, intended to make schools more accountable; and Medicare prescription drug laws, aimed at lowering costs for senior citizens.

Hillary Clinton: A former First Lady of the United States, Clinton also served as New York's junior senator from 2001 to 2009. Under President Barack Obama, Clinton served as secretary of state beginning in early 2009.

Simon Cowell: A British music executive, Cowell was one of the original judges on the hugely success TV show *American Idol,* which debuted in 2002. Known for his direct, honest, and, sometimes cruel comments to contestants, Cowell helped make the program one of the most popular in television history.

Eminem: A rap star and producer whose hit albums include *The Marshall Mathers LP* and the Grammy-winning *The Eminem Show.* In late 2009 Eminem was named the Artist of the Decade by *Billboard* magazine.

Bill Gates and Melinda Gates: Founders in 1994 of the Bill and Melinda Gates Foundation, which is dedicated to improving health care and fighting extreme poverty around the world. By 2009 its endowment had grown to more than $33 billion, making it the largest private foundation in the world. Bill Gates is the founder of Microsoft.

Saddam Hussein: The former dictator of the Middle Eastern nation of Iraq, Hussein goaded his enemies into war during the 1990s. In 2003 American forces invaded the country and overthrew Hussein's regime. He was captured, put on trial, and convicted of mass murder in 2003. Three years later he was hanged.

Michael Jackson: A Grammy-winning, multi-platinum-selling singer, songwriter, and record producer. Known by the nickname "the King of Pop," Jackson's immense popularity declined during the 2000s. After his death in June 2009, his albums again reached the top of the charts.

Steve Jobs: Cofounder and chief executive officer of Apple, Jobs helped pioneer two popular consumer products in the 2000s: the iPod and iPhone.

Khalid Sheikh Mohammed: The mastermind behind the 9/11 attacks on the United States, Mohammed, along with Osama bin Laden, planned the hijacking of airplanes and the subsequent acts of terrorism that led to the murders of nearly 3,000 people. He was captured by Pakistani forces in 2003.

Michael Moore: A controversial documentary filmmaker, Moore's films include *Sicko*, about health care in the United States, and *Fahrenheit 9/11*, about the Bush administration's response to the terrorist attacks of September 11, 2001.

Barack Obama: The forty-fourth president of the United States, elected in November 2008. A former community organizer and senator, Obama was the first African American ever elected to the high office.

Sandra Day O'Connor: The first woman to sit on the Supreme Court, O'Connor remained a moderate voice on the bench until her retirement in 2005.

Sarah Palin: A former Republican governor of Alaska, Palin was chosen as presidential candidate John McCain's running mate in 2008. Palin's shoot-from-the-hip style endeared her to millions of Republican voters, but others questioned her viability as a candidate for one of the nation's highest offices.

Nancy Pelosi: A California congresswoman, Pelosi became the first female Speaker of the House of Representatives in January 2007.

David Petraeus: A four-star US Army general whose command is credited with helping stabilize the country of Iraq in the late 2000s.

Pope Benedict XVI: The 265th pope of the Roman Catholic Church, elected in 2005. He succeeded Pope John Paul II.

Pope John Paul II: The second-longest-serving pope of the Roman Catholic Church. He died in 2005.

Nicolas Sarkozy: President of France, Sarkozy was elected in 2007.

Jon Stewart: Began hosting *The Daily Show* on the Comedy Central network in the late 1990s. By the 2000s, Stewart had become a respected progressive voice who used satire and humor to uncover political hypocrisy.

For Further Research

Books

Ken Auletta, *Googled: The End of the World as We Know It.* New York: Penguin, 2010.

Thomas L. Friedman, *Hot, Flat, and Crowded 2.0: Why We Need a Green Revolution—and How It Can Renew America.* New York: Picador, 2009.

Leander Kahney, *Inside Steve's Brain.* New York: Portfolio, 2009.

Hazel Rose Markus and Paula M.L. Moya, *Doing Race: 21 Essays for the 21st Century.* New York: W.W. Norton, 2010.

William Roe Polk, *Understanding Iran: Everything You Need to Know, from Persia to the Islamic Republic, from Cyrus to Ahmadinejad.* New York: Palgrave Macmillan, 2009.

David Remnick, *The Bridge: The Life and Rise of Barack Obama.* New York: Knopf, 2010.

Bernie Trilling and Charles Fadel, *21st Century Skills: Learning for Life in Our Times.* San Fransisco: Jossey-Bass, 2009.

William M. Wallace, *The Decline and Fall of the U.S. Economy: How Liberals and Conservatives Both Got It Wrong.* New York: Praeger, 2010.

Lawrence Wright, *The Looming Tower: Al-Qaeda and the Road to 9/11.* New York: Vintage, 2007.

Fareed Zakaria, *The Post-American World.* New York: W.W. Norton, 2009.

Websites

End of the Decade (www.abcnews.go.com/US/Decade). This fun site takes users on a tour of many of the most important news stories of the 2000s. From the premiere of *American Idol* to Janet Jackson's wardrobe "malfunction" at Super Bowl XXXVII, the site is navigated by moving an image of the ball that drops to ring in each New Year in Times Square.

Ten Science Stories That Changed Our Decade (http://io9.com/54 30073/ten-science-stories-that-changed-our-decade). For the science-minded, this site highlights the decade's top science stories, including the mapping of the human genome, climate change, and the development of "supercrafts" that may soon be flying the friendly skies.

The Top Pop Artists of the Decade—the 2000s (www.popeater.com/ 2009/12/09/top-pop-artists-of-the-decade-2000s). Popeater presents a fascinating, video-supported look at the pop culture icons of the 2000s. From the resurgence of Green Day to the ongoing saga that is Britney Spears, the site provides a rundown of the celebrities people love to love and love to hate.

2000s: The Decade in Sports (www.sportsillustrated.cnn.com/2009/ magazine/specials/2000s/12/20/decade.index/index.html). For sports fans, this *Sports Illustrated* site is an exceptional look back at the highs and lows of athletic competition during the millennial decade. It is chock-full of action-packed photos and in-depth articles about super-stars like Tiger Woods, Serena and Venus Williams, and A-Rod, to name but a few.

Worst Movies of the Decade (www.rottentomatoes.com/guides/worst_ of_the_worst). Find the best movies of the 2000s and put them on your Netflix list, but if you want to have a bit more fun, check out this website and countdown of the top 100 worst movies of the decade as voted on by movie critics. From *Battlefield Earth* to *Superbabies: Baby Geniuses 2*, movie lovers can see just how low these bad movies can go.

Index

Picture Credits

David Robson's many books for young readers include *Disaster Response* and *The Kennedy Assassination*. He is also an award-winning playwright, whose work for the stage has been performed across the country and abroad. He lives in Wilmington, Delaware, with his family.